Okanagan Eats

OKANAGAN EATS

Signature Chefs' Recipes
from British Columbia's Wine Valleys

DAWN POSTNIKOFF AND JOANNE SASVARI

PHOTOGRAPHY BY JON ADRIAN

Figure 1

Vancouver / Toronto / Berkeley

Dedicated to the growers and the makers. Without you, there would be no food on our plates, wine in our glasses or words on these pages. Thank you.

Cataloguing data is available from Library and Archives Canada
ISBN 978-1-77327-180-4 (hbk.)

Interior design by Teresa Bubela
Cover design by Naomi MacDougall
Photography by Jon Adrian, except p. 114 by Sophia Hsin
Prop styling by Tara Reavie + Jenny Adrian
Food styling by Jenny Adrian
Assistance by Candice Wahler

Editing by Michelle Meade
Copy editing by Pam Robertson
Proofreading by Breanne MacDonald
Indexing by Iva Cheung

Printed and bound in China by Printplus Ltd., Hong Kong (China)
Distributed internationally by Publishers Group West

Figure 1 Publishing Inc.
Vancouver B.C. Canada
www.figure1publishing.com

Figure 1 Publishing works in the traditional, unceded territory of the xʷməθkʷəy̓əm (Musqueam), Sḵwx̱wú7mesh (Squamish), and səlilwətaɬ (Tsleil-Waututh) peoples.

RECIPE NOTES

Unless stated otherwise:
Butter is unsalted.
Citrus juices are freshly squeezed.
Eggs are large.
Flour is all-purpose.
Herbs are fresh.
Milk is whole.
Pepper is black and freshly ground.
Produce is medium-sized.
Salt is kosher (not coarse).
Sugar is granulated.

CONTENTS

INTRODUCTION

Chefs the world over talk about dining with the seasons. But in the Okanagan, Thompson and Similkameen Valleys, they talk about the *micro-seasons*—those few short days when cherries or tomatoes or wild asparagus are at absolute peak ripeness, when their fragrance is intoxicating and when their flavour simply explodes on your tongue. Just ask anyone who's bitten into an heirloom peach plucked from an Okanagan tree in August. It's so sweet and juicy and quintessentially peachy, it's practically life-changing.

Indeed, it *has* been life-changing for many of the chefs on these pages. So many of them have relocated from big cities and celebrated kitchens, drawn to this region by the incredible abundance of what grows here. That could mean the cattle that graze the grasslands of the Thompson River Valley, the freshwater fish of the Shuswap, the organic tomatoes and peppers of the Similkameen, or the apples and apricots of the Okanagan.

And the vines are everywhere, heavy with grapes, because this is wine country, too.

The Thompson-Okanagan is a land of varied landscapes formed by cataclysmic events, volcanos, glaciers and raging rivers that carved steep valleys out of rock. It is also a land of varied climates that range from cool, green Lake Country in the north to the blistering desert of the South Okanagan Valley just 150 kilometres away.

The region comprises three valleys: two river valleys—the Similkameen and Thompson—and the Okanagan Valley, where a series of lakes travel north from the U.S. border. Some 12,000 years ago, the whole area was buried under ice and that era of glaciation has left behind the kinds of mineral, rock, sand, silt and other deposits that make soil scientists giddy with excitement. Not surprisingly, then, this has long been farming and ranching country. Even today, while cities like Kamloops and Kelowna grow bigger and bigger, more than 8 percent of the region is still locked in the Agricultural Land Reserve.

But long before the first orchard was planted, this was for millennia home to the Syilx, Nlaka'pamux and Secwépemc peoples who fished, hunted and foraged here. Europeans began to arrive in the early 1800s, drawn first by the fur trade and later by gold, especially during the Fraser River Gold Rush that began in 1858. These newcomers started farming and ranching and set up shop to supply optimistic prospectors. In 1859, three Oblate missionaries led by Father Charles Pandosy established the first European settlement in what is now Kelowna, where they also planted the region's first grapevines. By the dawn of the twentieth century, steamboats plied the waters of Okanagan Lake, transporting orchard fruits to the national railway and bringing tourists down to the beaches of the sunny Okanagan.

For a long time, this was "peaches and beaches" country, with just a handful of wineries growing mainly hybrid grapes like Vidal and Maréchal Foch. Then, in the 1980s, a series of international trade agreements opened the market for wine. The federal government paid growers to tear out their hybrid grapes and replace them with *Vitis vinifera*, the noble grapes that go into the world's great wines. Now there are more than two hundred wineries across the region, with more opening all the time.

And as the wineries began to win international awards and plant more and more acres of vines, the food scene grew alongside.

Mission Hill Family Estate Winery (page 166) led the charge, winning B.C.'s first international award for wine in 1994 and opening one of the region's first winery restaurants in 2002. Owner Anthony von Mandl was inspired by what Robert Mondavi was doing in the Napa Valley, where the patriarch of California wine combined wine, art, music, food and the fine craft of living well. That quickly became the model for the Okanagan Valley, too, as winery after winery opened its own restaurant, more stand-alone restaurants followed and chefs started leaving larger cities for a place where abundance is simply a way of life.

Now each part of this region is creating its own culinary culture. The Similkameen Valley is still mainly farm country, a deep, narrow, winding valley where rocky soils and dry winds create perfect conditions for organic farming. The Crowsnest Highway as it passes through Cawston and Keremeos is still lined with family-owned fruit stands that have been passed down from generation to generation. Dining here is casual, and profoundly ingredient led.

To the north, the Shuswap is famous for its summertime houseboating scene and its many golf courses. This is cool-climate wine country—the first winery opened in 1997—with a small but growing food scene driven by producers making cheese, raising bison or developing sustainable aquaculture.

And to the west, the North and South Thompson Rivers meet at Kamloops, which is also the confluence of Highways 1, 5 and 97. For a long time, this was known mainly as a place to stop for a burger or a double-double as you travelled through town. But in 2010, the first brew pub opened, followed in 2012 by the first winery—and suddenly "the Loops" had a dynamic restaurant scene of its own.

Dining in the Thompson-Okanagan is rarely fussy or fancy. But look a little closer and you will see serious skill on each plate. The region's chefs are quietly bringing world-class techniques to the table, taking the golden beets, tomatillos, wild mushrooms, haskap berries—and everything that grows so abundantly in every micro-season—and transforming it all into the kinds of meals that would tickle a Michelin reviewer's palate.

Then again, like us, sometimes they are happy just to eat a peach.

WINE VALLEYS

A Conversation with Naramata Inn
Wine Director Emily Walker

It's impossible to talk about the food of the Thompson-Okanagan without also talking about the wine. These are some of the most exciting wine regions in the world, unique in so many ways, from the climate to the soil to the people who work it so passionately. And few people are as well placed to explain what makes these regions so significant as Emily Walker, the wine director at the Naramata Inn (page 108).

Unlike most fine-dining restaurants in wine country, the one at the inn isn't attached to a winery, which gives Walker the opportunity to share wines from all over British Columbia and around the world. As a result, she has prime access to rare bottlings, historic library wines and kooky one-offs that few sommeliers get to taste. And because local winemakers and growers are her guests as well as her suppliers, she gets all the dirt on, well, the dirt.

"Our wine region is on the very edge of where grape-growing is possible," she says. "We're a region of extremes."

The fiftieth parallel of latitude, north or south of the equator, is considered the outer region where quality grape-growing is possible. The northern one runs through both Lake Country and Kamloops. Meanwhile, the forty-ninth parallel at our southern border is further north than Burgundy. As a result, B.C. is considered a cool-climate region, but, as Walker points out, "We don't fit into the definition of cool climate because of our hot summers. In a normal year, it's not uncommon for us to break 40° Celsius in Osoyoos, and it's not uncommon to have a thirty-degree shift in a day—that same vineyard can be 8° Celsius at night."

There are two major effects of this mix of northern location and huge temperature swings. "One benefit of being this far north is the extra sunlight. We need those extra hours of sunlight, because our growing season is so compact," Walker says. For instance, bud break in B.C. occurs weeks, sometimes months, after it does in California, but we are able to harvest at the same time, thanks to all that extra daylight.

The second major impact—the huge temperature swing—is what is known as the diurnal temperature shift. "Those lovely cool nights retain freshness and acidity along with those beautiful aromatics."

It's not just the climate that makes this a unique wine-growing region. It's also geography and geology. Virtually all of the Thompson-Okanagan's vineyards are located on glacial sediment, although some are also on volcanic soil, ancient seabeds and/or alluvial fans. It's a mix of soils that is rare, if not unique, on the planet.

Some 12,000 years ago, during the last ice age, Glacial Lake Penticton filled the Okanagan Valley—its shoreline was just above where Naramata Road is now—with an ice dam blocking it at McIntyre Bluff. At one point, the dam burst, and the lake flooded what is now the South Okanagan. "It has been described as quite a catastrophic event that dispersed all the sediment and minerals all over the valley," Walker says.

It left behind the lakes (Okanagan, Skaha, Vaseux, Osoyoos) that moderate the valley temperatures, as well as the "kettled" area of Okanagan Falls (its hills and divots caused by giant ice boulders sent flying when the dam burst) and the wider, flatter areas around Osoyoos and Oliver. It also left layer upon layer of mineral-rich soils. "We have a huge diversity of soil types," Walker says.

Meanwhile, the Thompson and Similkameen Valleys are close to the Okanagan in terms of distance, but different in almost every other way. Both are east-west valleys (rather than north-south), following rivers rather than lakes: the north and south branches of the Thompson are wide, relatively straight and slow-moving; the Similkameen is narrow, wild and twisty. The Similkameen Valley is likewise narrow and steep, its calcium-carbonate-rich soil, high daytime temperatures and brisk winds producing lush, boldly flavoured wines. The arid grasslands of the North Thompson Valley, on the other hand, are built on ancient flood plains, with a bed of limestone and volcanic rock that adds a complex minerality to wines.

These are conditions with the potential to grow some of the best wine in the world. But it takes people to make it happen.

British Columbia is a very young wine region. Although the first vines were planted here in 1859 and the first commercial winery opened in 1932, the wine industry really only dates to 1990 and the formation of the Vintners Quality Alliance and the B.C. Wine Institute (now Wine Growers B.C.). Today there are some 186 wineries and 10,000 acres planted in the Okanagan, with another 15 wineries in the Similkameen, 8 in the Shuswap and 5 in the Thompson Valley.

There has been an enormous increase in quality over the last decade or so, and alongside it, an equally great increase in sustainable wine-growing and wine-making practices. Some 20 percent of the Okanagan's wine-growing area is now certified organic. In most wine regions, it's less than 2 percent. And all of this has led to a unique style of wine in a unique region.

Our wines, Walker says, have "interesting aromatics, flavour intensity and complexity from sunlight, coupled with freshness, acidity and a bright profile. These two things—bold flavour and bright acidity—rarely go together except in very high-quality wine."

This is a region right on the edge, it turns out, not just of where wine can be made, but of producing some of the world's greatest wines.

THE RESTAURANTS

THE RECIPES

15 PARK BISTRO
AT WATERMARK BEACH RESORT

Nick Atkins
OSOYOOS

Even in a valley with plenty of spectacular locations, the Watermark Beach Resort is in an especially enviable spot: right on the shores of Canada's warmest lake and just steps from charming downtown Osoyoos. This is where you will find 15 Park Bistro, a bright, modern dining room that sprawls out onto a patio where happy guests sip wine and savour chef Nick Atkins's upscale casual cuisine.

Hailing from Calgary, Atkins has competed in international culinary competitions and worked at the legendary fine-dining establishment La Chaumière before joining the Vintage Group. But by 2020, he'd started a young family and was looking for a new challenge. The Okanagan beckoned.

"I had a friend out here who knew I was looking for work," he recalls. "We're outdoorsy people so we thought, yeah, sure."

The owners of the resort were planning a major rebrand of their dark, crowded restaurant, and Atkins was the perfect fit for the new cheerfully contemporary room. "We wanted to bring casual fine-dining to the South Okanagan," Atkins says. "We wanted to make every dish stand out, for everything to have a 'wow' factor. And we wanted to offer something entirely different in the area."

That led to the creation of the valley's only lobster bar, while the rest of the menu follows the seasons and relies on produce from nearby farms. The dynamic wine list features mostly labels from the Okanagan and Similkameen—perfect for sitting and sipping on that gorgeous lakeside patio.

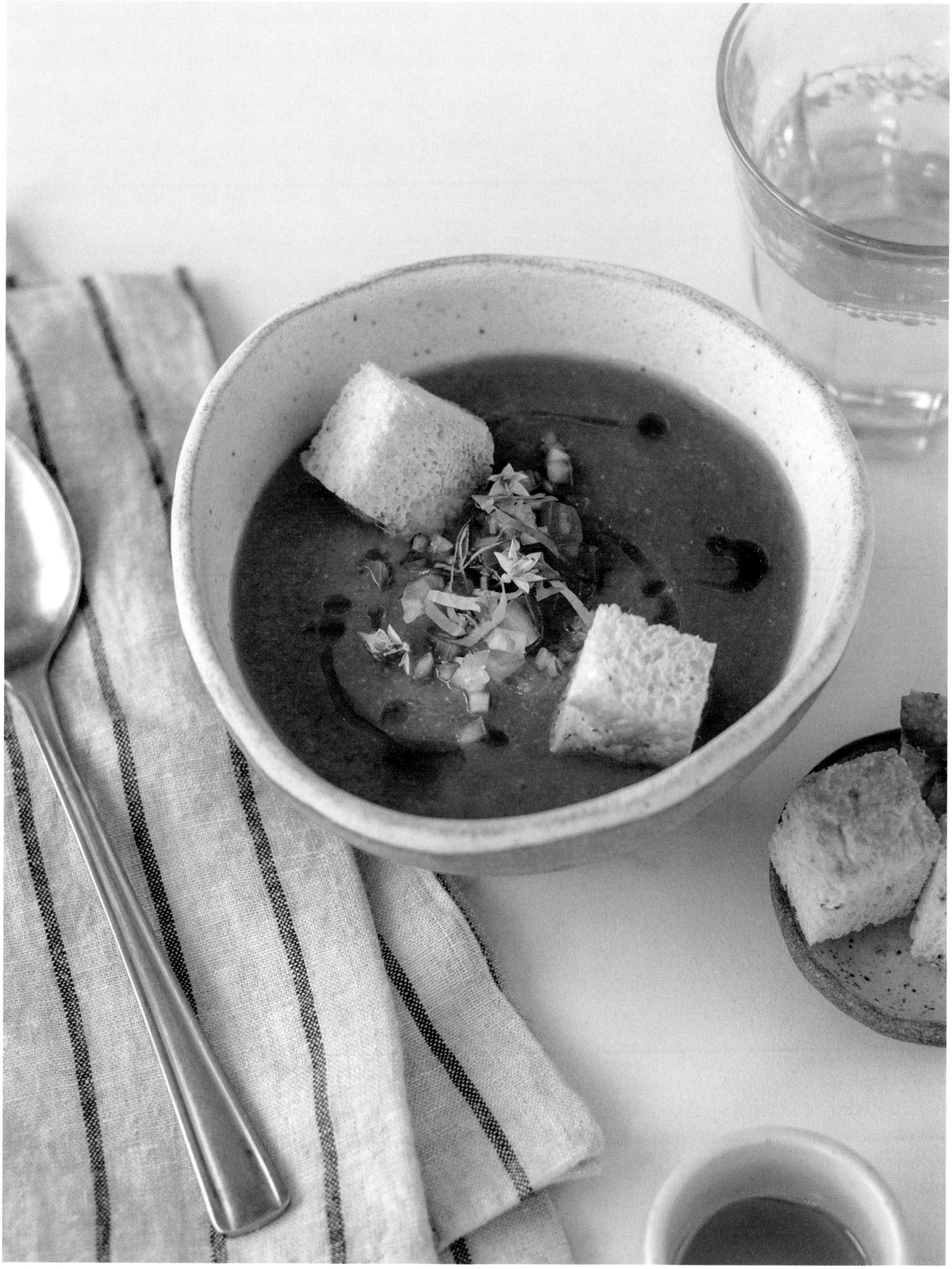

Heirloom Tomato Gazpacho, p. 20

Heirloom Tomato Gazpacho

The Similkameen Valley is famous for its tomatoes. They shine in chef Nick Atkins's chilled soup, perfect for days when the temperature soars—as it does so often here in the South Okanagan. Fresh cucumber, peppers, onions and spices add complexity, while the basil oil and salsa fresca garnishes transform this gazpacho into something extraordinary. SERVES 4

Lariana Cellars
Viognier

GAZPACHO

1 green bell pepper

4 thick slices day-old bread, such as herb focaccia (divided)

3 lbs heirloom tomatoes, cored, seeded and chopped

1 English cucumber, peeled, seeded and roughly chopped

2 cloves garlic

½ red onion, roughly chopped

1 to 2 tsp salt

1 tsp black pepper

1 tsp ground cumin

2 Tbsp Worcestershire sauce

1 Tbsp sherry vinegar

5 drops Tabasco sauce

Juice of ½ lemon

GAZPACHO Preheat oven to 350°F.

Preheat a flame grill over high heat. Roast green pepper over open flame until charred on all sides. Place pepper in a bowl, then cover with plastic wrap and set aside for 4 minutes. Remove burnt skin, stem and seeds.

Cut 2 slices of bread into 1-inch cubes. Arrange on a baking sheet and toast for 3 to 5 minutes, turning often, until just crisp on the outside but soft on the inside. Set aside.

Place the roasted green pepper and all remaining ingredients, including the remaining 2 slices of bread, into a blender and blend until combined. If needed, adjust seasoning.

Chill soup in the fridge for at least 2 hours. Soup can be made the day before serving. Croutons can be stored in an air-tight container until ready to serve.

BASIL OIL

2 cups canola oil

2¾ cups basil leaves (2 oz)

SALSA FRESCA

2 Roma tomatoes, finely chopped

1 Tbsp finely chopped red onions

1 Tbsp chopped cilantro, or to taste

1 jalapeño, finely chopped

1 tsp salt

1 tsp black pepper

Juice of ½ lime

ASSEMBLY

Croutons, for garnish (see here)

Edible flowers, for garnish (optional)

BASIL OIL Heat oil in a small but deep saucepan to a temperature of 325°F. Carefully lower basil into pan. (The oil will pop and sizzle once the basil leaves make contact with the oil.) Fry for 10 to 15 seconds, taking care not to let the leaves brown. Using a slotted spoon, transfer basil to a paper towel–lined plate to drain. It will crisp up when you remove it from the oil. Set aside pan until oil is completely cooled.

Transfer oil and basil to a high-power blender or food processor and blend until smooth and vibrant green. Strain oil through a coffee filter and set aside.

Leftover basil oil can be stored in the fridge for up to a month. It's great on salads, pastas and pizzas, or drizzled over a tomato and burrata salad.

SALSA FRESCA Combine all ingredients and set aside.

ASSEMBLY Divide the chilled soup among soup bowls. Top with a generous spoonful of salsa fresca, then add a few drops of basil oil and garnish with croutons and edible flowers (if using).

Wild Mushroom and Goat Cheese Quiche with Spring Salad

A perfect light lunch or brunch dish, this quiche from chef Nick Atkins is rich with a seasonal medley of sautéed mushrooms—morels, chanterelles and/or whatever you can forage at your local grocery store—along with creamy goat cheese in a made-from-scratch pastry shell. Serve it with a simple salad dressed with a refreshing citrus and white balsamic vinaigrette. SERVES 8

vinAmitè
Chardonnay

PASTRY

1 egg

2½ Tbsp ice water

1½ cups flour, plus extra for dusting

½ tsp salt

½ cup + 2 Tbsp (1¼ sticks) cold butter, cubed

FILLING

3 Tbsp canola oil

1 lb button mushrooms, quartered

½ lb mushrooms, such as morel, chanterelle and/or oyster (see Note)

4 cloves garlic, finely chopped

2 shallots, thinly sliced

2 Tbsp finely chopped herbs, such as thyme, rosemary, parsley and/or chives

¼ cup dry white wine

5 eggs

1⅔ cups heavy (36%) cream

Salt and black pepper, to taste

3 oz creamy goat cheese

PASTRY In a small mixing bowl, whisk together egg and ice water. Chill until needed.

In a food processor, combine flour and salt and pulse briefly to mix. Add butter and pulse until mixture forms pea-sized crumbs. Add the egg-water mixture and pulse again until a dough forms.

Transfer the dough to a lightly floured surface. Roll out the dough into a disk, about 11 inches in diameter and ¼ inch thick. Roll dough around your rolling pin and carefully unroll it over the quiche pan.

Gently press the dough into place using your hands. Drape excess dough over edge and use a sharp knife to trim the edges. Dock the base of the pastry a few times with a fork. Refrigerate for at least 1 hour and up to overnight. Alternatively, place quiche pan in the freezer for 30 minutes. (A cold dough will result in a nice flaky crust when it is blind baked; if it is too warm, the butter will run out.)

Preheat oven to 350°F. Place quiche pan on a baking sheet. Crumple a sheet of parchment paper so it becomes pliable and position over the dough, making sure the edges are covered, then fill with pie weights or dry beans. Bake for 12 minutes. Remove from oven and remove parchment and weights. Bake for another 5 minutes. Set aside to cool.

FILLING Heat oil in a frying pan over medium heat. Add all mushrooms and sauté for 10 to 15 minutes, until golden brown. Add garlic and shallots and sauté for 2 minutes. Stir in herbs, then deglaze with wine and cook until all the liquid has evaporated.

In a medium bowl, beat eggs with cream. Season with a pinch of salt and pepper.

Pour mushroom mixture into the quiche crust and spread out evenly. Dot with goat cheese, then pour in egg-cream mixture.

Place quiche pan on a baking sheet and bake for 50 minutes, or until the centre is barely jiggly and the top is puffed and golden brown. A knife inserted into the centre should come out clean.

NOTE Dried mushrooms may also be used. Just be sure to soak in hot water for 15 minutes first.

Grated zest and juice
  of 1 orange

Grated zest and juice
  of 1 lemon

Grated zest and juice
  of 1 lime

¼ cup white balsamic
  vinegar

1 Tbsp honey

1 Tbsp Dijon mustard

¾ cup olive oil

Salt and black pepper,
  to taste

4 cups artisan lettuce,
  such as red leaf,
  green leaf, radicchio,
  frisée or a mix,
  hand torn

12 cherry tomatoes,
  halved, for garnish

2 Tbsp toasted
  pumpkin seeds,
  for garnish

TO SERVE In a food processor, combine all of the citrus zest and juice with the vinegar, honey and mustard. With the motor still running, gradually add oil and blend until emulsified. Season to taste with salt and pepper.

Place lettuce in a large bowl. Add dressing and toss lightly. Divide salad among individual plates. Garnish with cherry tomatoes and toasted pumpkin seeds. Add a slice of quiche to each plate and serve.

19 BISTRO
AT FITZPATRICK FAMILY VINEYARDS

Merissa Hucul, Neil Martens and Geoff Molloy

PEACHLAND

It wasn't, perhaps, the most promising way to begin a friendship.

It was 5:45 p.m. on the crazy-busy Friday before a long weekend when someone dropped in to see Neil Martens, owner of 19 Okanagan Grill + Bar in West Kelowna. "I didn't realize it was Gordon Fitzpatrick—I assumed it was some random delivery guy and I asked if he always delivered on a Friday afternoon of a long weekend." He laughs. "We've gotten along since that moment."

Back then, Fitzpatrick was still president of CedarCreek Estate Winery. In 2017, he opened Fitzpatrick Family Vineyards, specializing in sparkling wines, on his family's Greata Ranch property in Peachland. And this location demanded a restaurant where guests could savour its stunning lake view. So Fitzpatrick turned to Martens and his team, assistant general manager Merissa Hucul and head chef Geoff Molloy. They opened 19 Bistro in 2021.

Molloy, who was born and raised in the Okanagan Valley, describes his food as "adventurous, but not." At 19 Bistro, he explores his love of Asian flavours (which go so well with bubbles) and uses local products in a way he can't at the high-volume bar and grill. "That's the beauty of the Okanagan. Everyone is doing something cool here," he says. "It's great to be able to support local farmers. I like people giving me random products and seeing what I can do with them."

Adds Hucul, "The Fitzpatrick brand is sophisticated ease. We want to be approachable but deliver an amazing food experience and good service. We want people to feel comfortable stopping by in their jeans."

Besides, there's that view. "It's outrageous, really," Hucul says.

Baked Brie with Haskap-Jalapeño Jam

Nothing pairs more beautifully with a crisp sparkling wine than a rich, creamy brie—except maybe one that is baked until rich and luscious, and enjoyed on the winery's patio overlooking Okanagan Lake. Here, chef Geoff Molloy adds a lightly spiced jam made with tart, local haskap berries to give it some zing. SERVES 4 TO 6

Fitzpatrick Family Vineyards Fitz Crémant Sparkling Wine

CANDIED ALMONDS

⅓ cup high-quality maple syrup, such as Maple Roch

½ tsp Thai red curry paste

1 tsp sea salt

¾ cup raw almonds, blanched

HASKAP-JALAPEÑO JAM

8 oz fresh or frozen haskap berries or blueberries (divided)

½ jalapeño, seeded, stemmed and finely chopped

6 Tbsp sugar

1 tsp agar-agar (see Note)

⅓ cup water

BAKED BRIE

1 tsp olive oil, plus extra for greasing

½ baguette

Salt and black pepper, to taste

1 small wheel brie

2 Tbsp Haskap-Jalapeño Jam (see here)

8 Candied Almonds (see here), for garnish

¼ cup microgreens or arugula, dressed with olive oil, salt and pepper, for garnish

Local crackers, such as Raincoast Crisps, to serve (optional)

CANDIED ALMONDS Preheat oven to 350°F. Line a baking sheet with parchment paper.

In a mixing bowl, whisk together maple syrup, curry paste and salt. Stir in almonds, then spread evenly on the prepared baking sheet. Bake for 15 to 20 minutes, until golden brown. Remove from oven and set aside to cool.

Leftover almonds can be stored in an airtight container for up to 3 months.

HASKAP-JALAPEÑO JAM Meanwhile, in a medium saucepan, combine half the berries with the jalapeños, sugar, agar-agar and water. Mix well. Bring to a simmer over medium heat and cook for 5 minutes, until thickened. Remove from heat. Transfer mixture to a small food processor and blend until smooth. Add the remaining 4 ounces of berries and set aside to cool. Makes 1½ cups.

Leftover jam can be stored in an airtight container for up to 2 weeks in the fridge. Enjoy with your next cheese or charcuterie board.

NOTE Agar-agar, known simply as agar in culinary circles, is a plant-based gelatin derived from seaweed.

BAKED BRIE Preheat oven to 400°F. Grease a baking sheet generously with oil or line with parchment paper.

Slice the baguette into rounds, cutting just three-quarters of the way through. (This makes it easier to pull apart once warmed.) Brush with oil, then season with salt and pepper. Place it on one side of the baking sheet. Add brie to the other side and top with haskap-jalapeño jam. Bake for 7 minutes, until brie has softened in the centre and baguette is golden brown.

Transfer brie to a large serving plate. Arrange almonds and microgreens on top. Place baguette on one side of the plate and fan crackers (if using) along the other side. Serve immediately.

Seafood Fettuccine

A perfect partner to a crisp dry white wine, still or sparkling, this rich and luxurious pasta dish from chef Geoff Molloy makes an excellent dinner-party main. Lemongrass gives it an almost floral citrus flavour—and its delicate fragrance is complemented by the wine and balanced out by the cream. This is one dish worth opening the bubbly for. SERVES 2

Fitzpatrick Family Vineyards Fitz Crémant Sparkling Wine

OVEN-ROASTED CHERRY TOMATOES

20 cherry tomatoes (about 1 cup)

1 tsp salt

1 tsp black pepper

2 Tbsp olive oil

LEMONGRASS CREAM SAUCE

¼ cup canola oil

4 cloves garlic, finely chopped

2 stalks lemongrass, outer layers removed and paler sections finely chopped

1 shallot, finely chopped

½ cup Fitzpatrick Lookout Riesling

2 cups whipping (33%) cream

½ cup vegetable stock

1 Tbsp soy sauce

Grated zest and juice of 1 lemon

1 cup loosely packed basil leaves

ASSEMBLY

2 Tbsp salt

1 Tbsp olive oil

200 g high-quality dried fettuccine

¼ cup canola oil

8 extra-large prawns (16/20 count), shelled and deveined

Salt and black pepper, to taste

½ lb fresh Dungeness crabmeat, picked of shells or cartilage and cooked

Grated zest and juice of 1 lemon

3 basil leaves, torn, for garnish

1 serrano pepper, seeded and thinly sliced, for garnish (optional)

OVEN-ROASTED CHERRY TOMATOES Preheat broiler. Combine all ingredients in a mixing bowl and mix well. Spread out on a baking sheet. Broil for 5 minutes, until tomatoes blister. Set aside to cool.

LEMONGRASS CREAM SAUCE Heat oil in a saucepan over medium heat. Add garlic, lemongrass and shallots and sauté for 5 minutes, until shallots are translucent. Deglaze with wine and cook for another 10 minutes, until reduced by half.

Stir in cream, stock, soy sauce, lemon zest and juice, and basil. Cook for 10 minutes, stirring occasionally, until thickened and reduced by half. Using an immersion blender, blend until smooth.

ASSEMBLY Add the salt and olive oil to a stockpot of water and bring it to a rolling boil over medium-high heat. Add pasta and cook according to package directions until al dente. Drain.

Meanwhile, heat canola oil in a large frying pan over medium heat. Add prawns and sear for 1 minute on each side, until golden brown. Add oven-roasted tomatoes and stir until heated through. Pour in cream sauce and simmer for 1 minute.

Stir in cooked pasta, then season to taste with salt and black pepper. Divide between 2 bowls and arrange prawns on top.

In a small bowl, combine crab and lemon zest and juice. Divide evenly on top of each bowl. Garnish with torn basil and serrano pepper slices (if using).

THE BISTRO AT HILLSIDE WINERY

Evan Robertson

NARAMATA

Back when chef Evan Robertson was still living in Calgary and cooking at the award-winning Market on 17th Avenue, he and his wife would "make an annual pilgrimage to the Okanagan" and dream of living there—someday.

Then COVID-19 hit and his restaurant closed. "That fast-tracked things," he says. "I cold-called five restaurants in the Okanagan where I wanted to work—Hillside being No. 1—and sometimes dreams do come true."

In 2021, he joined Hillside, one of the oldest, most highly regarded wineries here on the Naramata Bench. Planted in 1984 with three and a half acres of vineyards, today the winery has twenty-five acres of Naramata-grown and -raised grapes. And in the skilled hands

of winemaker Kathy Malone, it's made a mark with its terroir-driven small-lot wines, especially its flagship Mosaic red blend.

It's also known for its terroir-to-table bistro, housed in a charming wooden building with a seventy-two-foot tower and two open-air patios—one with spectacular views of Okanagan Lake.

Because most of the dining is outdoors, the bistro is operated seasonally. But that suits Robertson fine, because he cooks in tune with the seasons and relies on relationships with local producers—something he learned early in his career at white-tablecloth establishments like The Aerie (now Villa Eyrie Resort) on Vancouver Island and the Hardware Grill in Edmonton.

"Now I'm building relationships with new producers in the Okanagan," he says. "It's gangbusters out here. It's a chef's paradise. Karla, my vegetable farmer, lives across the street at Plot Twist Farms. If I run out of lettuce at lunch service, I call her."

But despite his fine-dining roots, he keeps things real and unpretentious. "You shouldn't feel like you have to google everything on the menu," Robertson says. Instead, he wants you to feel like you belong. "I'd rather have people use their phones to take pictures of my dishes—or book a second reservation for tomorrow."

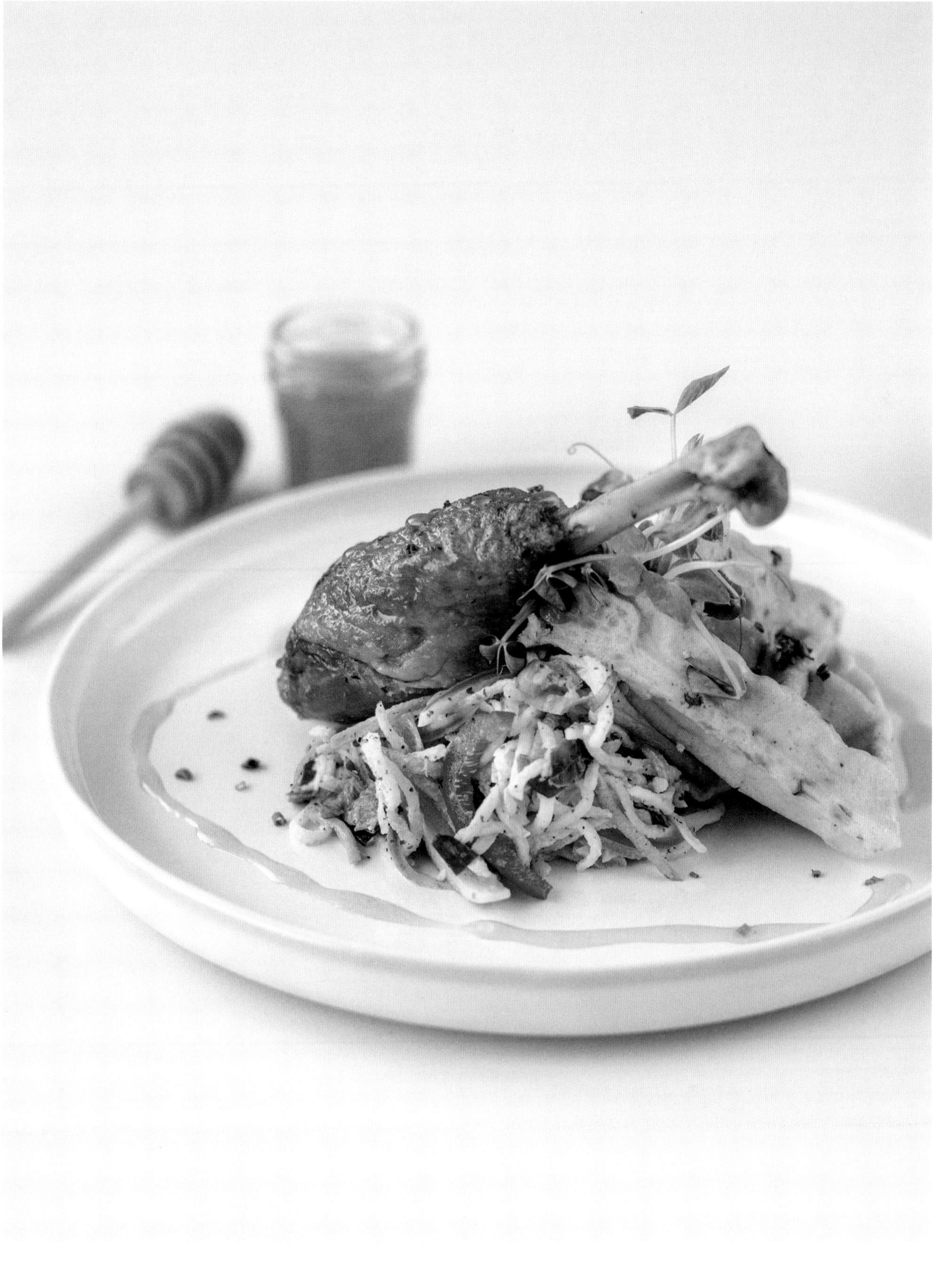

Duck and Waffles, p. 32

Duck and Waffles

At Hillside Bistro, chef Evan Robertson offers this dish as a great savoury lunch item, but it would also be an impressive centrepiece for a fancy brunch or a light dinner. Most of the components can be made ahead of time and assembled when needed. At the restaurant, it is served with a light and tangy kohlrabi coleslaw. SERVES 4

🍷 Hillside Winery
Gamay Noir

HERB SALT

4 bay leaves, crushed

1 cup salt

¼ cup brown sugar

½ cup chopped Italian parsley

¼ cup chopped thyme

2 tsp black peppercorns

DUCK CONFIT

4 duck legs, fat trimmed (see Note)

¼ cup garlic purée

¼ cup Herb Salt, plus extra if needed (see here)

6 Tbsp rendered duck fat, or up to 2 cups if needed

HERB SALT Combine all ingredients in a food processor and blend well.

DUCK CONFIT With scissors, trim excess skin near bottom of the duck legs and around edges, leaving at least a ¼-inch overhang of skin.

Rub garlic purée and 1 tablespoon of herb salt over each duck leg. Rub a little extra over the joint and the thicker parts.

Line a baking sheet with parchment paper. Place duck legs, flesh-side up, in a single layer on the prepared baking sheet and wrap the whole sheet tightly with plastic wrap. Place in the fridge and allow to cure for 24 hours.

Rinse the duck legs under cold running water. Pat dry.

If you are using an immersion circulator (sous vide), divide the duck legs between 2 vacuum bags and add 3 Tbsp rendered duck fat to each bag. Vacuum pack on medium and sous vide at 180°F for 8 hours. Transfer bags to an ice bath to stop cooking. (Alternatively, preheat oven to 225°F. Place duck legs in a non-reactive baking dish and pour enough melted duck fat over them to cover fully. Cover with a lid or aluminum foil and bake for 4 hours, until the meat is falling-off-the-bone tender.) Set aside.

WAFFLES

1½ lbs peeled and grated
  russet potatoes
1½ lbs peeled and grated
  sweet potatoes
1 Tbsp canola oil
6 Tbsp finely chopped
  red onions
1 Tbsp garlic purée
1¼ cups flour
6 Tbsp chopped oregano
2 Tbsp chopped chives
2 Tbsp baking powder
1 Tbsp salt
1 Tbsp black pepper
10 eggs
½ cup heavy (36%) cream
1¼ cups cooked wild rice
Cooking spray, as needed

TRUFFLE HONEY

1 Tbsp canola oil
¼ cup chopped garlic
¼ cup chopped red onions
¾ cup white wine vinegar
½ cup maple syrup
2 cups honey
½ tsp salt
2 Tbsp truffle oil
½ tsp xanthan gum

ASSEMBLY

Kohlrabi coleslaw, to serve
  (optional)
Pea shoots or microgreens,
  for garnish (optional)

WAFFLES Preheat oven to 180°F.

Bring a saucepan of water to a boil. Add the grated russet potatoes and cook for 4 to 6 minutes, until par-cooked. Drain, then rinse under cold running water and squeeze dry. Repeat with the sweet potatoes. Set both aside.

Heat oil in a frying pan over medium heat. Add onions and garlic purée and sauté for 3 to 5 minutes, until soft and lightly golden. Allow to cool to room temperature.

In a large bowl, combine flour, herbs, baking powder, salt and pepper. Whisk in the eggs and cream. Fold in russet potatoes, sweet potatoes, onion mixture and wild rice.

Heat a waffle iron and spray well with cooking spray. Using a 6-ounce ladle, ladle batter into waffle iron and cook for 6 minutes, until crisp and golden. Repeat with remaining batter. Keep waffles warm in the oven until needed.

TRUFFLE HONEY Heat oil in a medium saucepan over medium heat. Add garlic and onions and sauté for 7 minutes, or until soft and translucent. Reduce heat, if necessary, to prevent them from burning.

Add vinegar, maple syrup, honey and salt and bring to a boil. Boil until vinegar smell turns sweet, then remove from heat. Stir in truffle oil. Using an immersion blender, purée until smooth. Sift in xanthan gum and blend until thickened. Strain through a fine-mesh sieve.

ASSEMBLY Divide the waffles between 4 plates and drizzle truffle honey on top. Place duck legs next to waffles, bones pointing to the sky. If desired, garnish with pea shoots (or microgreens) and serve with kohlrabi coleslaw.

Cherry Pavlova Bure

Hillside Bistro executive chef Evan Robertson named this elegant dessert for "the fanciest Vancouver Canuck ever to skate for the franchise"— Pavel Bure. It uses one of the Okanagan Valley's most beloved orchard fruits, the cherry, which comes into season every year around July.

When making meringue, the key is to make absolutely sure not a particle of grease or egg yolk gets into the whites; otherwise, they will not stiffen. SERVES 8 TO 10

Hillside Winery
Kerner Icewine

MERINGUE SHELLS
8 egg whites, room temperature
2½ cups sugar
2 Tbsp vanilla paste
2 tsp lemon juice
1 Tbsp cornstarch

CHERRY PORT SAUCE
1 cup pitted cherries
½ cup Port
½ cup honey
½ cup red currant jelly
1 Tbsp lemon juice

MERINGUE SHELLS Preheat oven to 300°F. Using a pencil, draw 8 to 10 circles on a piece of parchment paper, each about 4½ inches in diameter. (We use a plastic lid from a deli container.) Place the paper, drawn-side down, on a baking sheet. (The circles will show through.)

In a stand mixer fitted with a whisk attachment, beat egg whites until stiff but not dry. (Alternatively, use a hand mixer and a mixing bowl.) Take care not to over-beat egg whites as they will lose volume and deflate when other ingredients are folded in. Gradually add 1 tablespoon sugar at a time, beating well after each addition. Beat until thick and glossy.

In a small bowl, combine vanilla paste, lemon juice and cornstarch and mix well. Gently fold into the beaten egg whites.

Spoon the meringue mixture onto each circle of the parchment paper. Working from the centre, spread it towards the edges of the circles, building the edge slightly and leaving a slight depression in the centre. Bake for 1 hour, until crisp but not browned. Remove from oven and cool completely on a wire rack.

Meringues can be stored in an airtight container for up to 5 days.

CHERRY PORT SAUCE Soak cherries in Port for at least 12 hours or overnight. Strain Port and set aside. Put cherries in a separate bowl.

In a small saucepan, combine the reserved Port with the honey, red currant jelly and lemon juice and simmer over medium heat for 15 minutes, or until reduced by two-thirds. Remove from heat and allow to cool slightly. Stir in cherries. Purée until smooth using an immersion blender and then pass through a fine-mesh sieve.

CHERRY CURD

¾ cup sugar

2 tsp cornstarch

6 egg yolks

4 eggs

1½ cups Cherry Port Sauce (see here)

½ cup lemon juice

¼ cup heavy (36%) cream

¾ cup (1½ sticks) cold butter, cut into ½-inch cubes

ASSEMBLY

Sprigs of mint, for garnish

CHERRY CURD Fill a medium saucepan with water, about 2 inches deep, and bring to a simmer over medium heat. Combine all ingredients except the butter in a heatproof metal bowl. Place bowl over saucepan and whisk briskly until mixture has thickened. Remove from heat.

Slowly whisk in butter, one piece at a time, until melted. Place a piece of plastic wrap directly on the curd (so it doesn't form a skin) and chill. The curd can be stored for up to 2 days in the fridge.

ASSEMBLY Spoon cherry curd into the centre of baked meringues and top each with a sprig of mint. Don't forget to smack the mint to release the oils!

BLOCK ONE RESTAURANT AT 50TH PARALLEL

Kevin Deavu

LAKE COUNTRY

North or south, the fiftieth parallel of latitude is considered the extreme edge of where quality wine can be grown (see page 12). And it just happens to pass through Lake Country, where "glamour farmers" Curtis Krouzel and Sheri-Lee Turner-Krouzel planted their first Pinot Noir vines in 2009.

Those vines were on ten acres of rocky, sun-soaked slope they'd been eyeing for a while, convinced that it could produce Grand Cru–style Pinot to compare with anything from Burgundy. Today they have fifty-five acres under vine, barrels full of awards, a stunning contemporary facility and the popular Block One Restaurant, where executive chef Kevin Deavu pairs their wines with equally well-crafted dishes. "We're striving for a Michelin star when they come to the Okanagan," he says.

Deavu had been working in kitchens "as long as I can remember," he says—for chains and hotels, steakhouses and resorts, in B.C. and in his home province of Alberta. But after COVID-19 hit, he found himself working as the corporate executive chef with Arterra Wines, which opened a whole new world. He honed his palate, earned his WSET Level 2, and now says, "It enhanced my ability to pair food and wine."

It also led him straight to 50th Parallel, where he is making fine food from local ingredients, including peaches from the heirloom trees on the property and produce from their two covered garden spaces. "Getting our garden going—it doesn't get more local," he says.

Deavu adds: "What excites me about 50th Parallel is, there are no restrictions. Sheri-Lee and Curtis just want your best foot forward. As Sheri-Lee says, 'You never miss your chance to sparkle.' I just want to continue to expand with the success they've had."

As a winery, 50th Parallel Estate is focused on doing a very few things very well. So is Deavu: "I think simplicity is key. There is beauty in simplicity."

Beetroot-Cured Salmon Mosaic and Charred Greens

This dramatic dish by Block One executive chef Kevin Deavu makes the most of one of B.C.'s most treasured ingredients— sockeye salmon—and transforms it into a work of art that looks just like a beautiful mosaic. At the restaurant, he garnishes it with crunchy puffed sorghum, pickled seeds and a drizzle of fennel oil, but it is delicious just as it is. SERVES 4

50th Parallel
Estate Pinot Noir

PINOT VINAIGRETTE
4 Tbsp 50th Parallel Estate Profile Pinot Noir
2 Tbsp maple syrup
½ Tbsp grainy Dijon mustard
¾ Tbsp red wine vinegar
⅓ cup grapeseed oil
⅓ cup extra-virgin olive oil
4 fresh blackberries
Pinch of salt and pepper

SALMON MOSAICS
1 (1-lb) sockeye salmon fillet, skin removed
1 cup (150 g) beetroot powder
2 navel oranges, finely zested
2 Tbsp coarse salt
25 g (about 8 sheets) dried nori

CHARRED GREENS
1 head radicchio
¼ cup olive oil
2 Tbsp ground sumac
1 tsp coarse salt
Juice of 1 lemon
1 romaine heart
3 Tbsp Pinot Vinaigrette, or to taste (see here)

PINOT VINAIGRETTE Add wine, maple syrup, Dijon mustard and red wine vinegar to a food processor and process until combined.

With the motor running, slowly pour the two oils into the vinaigrette. Once fully emulsified, turn the processor off and add the fresh blackberries. Pulse the processor until the blackberries are broken down but the vinaigrette is not completely smooth.

Season with salt and pepper, then set aside until needed. Makes about 1 cup.

SALMON MOSAICS On a baking sheet, lay out the salmon and evenly coat on all sides with the beetroot powder, orange zest and salt. Wrap the salmon tightly with plastic wrap, pressing it close so it is nice and tight with no air pockets. Leave to cure in the fridge for at least 2 hours, but no more than 12.

Remove cured salmon from fridge and gently rinse with cold water to remove any solids. Pat dry with a paper towel.

Place the nori in a food processor and blitz until it becomes a fine powder. Transfer the powder to a plate.

Slice the salmon fillet lengthwise in five or six even strips, then roll the strips in the nori powder until they are evenly coated.

Lay out a sheet of plastic wrap about 6 inches longer than the salmon pieces. Stack the coated salmon strips on the plastic wrap, then pull the plastic wrap over the salmon, rolling it tightly into a cylinder, making sure there are no air pockets.

Twist the ends together, like you would a candy wrapper.

Place the rolled salmon in a vacuum-sealed bag or wrap it tightly in foil, then cook sous vide for 30 minutes. Once it is ready, immediately drop the plastic-wrapped salmon into an ice bath to cool, and then refrigerate for at least 1 hour.

While it is still in the plastic wrap, slice the salmon into 4 equal discs, trimming off the uneven ends. Remove the plastic, then place the salmon mosaics in the centre of 4 plates.

CHARRED GREENS Preheat grill or barbecue to medium-high.

Halve and core the radicchio. In a medium bowl, toss the halves with oil, sumac and salt.

Once the grill is hot, place the seasoned radicchio on it and grill for 7 to 10 minutes, turning it every couple of minutes until it is charred on all sides. Just before pulling the radicchio off the grill, squeeze the fresh lemon juice over the halves, then remove and set aside.

Gently rip the romaine heart into generous-sized chunks. (If you prefer, you can first halve and lightly oil the romaine heart, then grill, turning occasionally.) Roughly chop the charred radicchio.

Toss the radicchio and romaine together with the vinaigrette and surround the salmon mosaics with the dressed greens.

Popcorn and Chardonnay Ice Cream Sundae with Sablé Breton, Sesame Miso Caramel, Caramel Popcorn and Vegan Meringue Shards

This has long been one of Block One's most popular desserts, and for good reason—popcorn and Chardonnay are a perfect marriage. Beyond that, it's a symphony of creamy, caramelly flavours and layered textures. You may be tempted to leave out some of the garnishes, and it will still be delicious, but the whole together is utterly *chef's kiss*. SERVES 4

🍷 50th Parallel Estate Chardonnay

POPCORN-CHARDONNAY ICE CREAM

1 Tbsp vegetable oil
⅓ cup popcorn kernels
½ cup 50th Parallel Estate Chardonnay
1 cup sugar
2 cups whipping (33%) cream
1½ cups milk
1 Tbsp vanilla extract
½ tsp salt
6 egg yolks

VEGAN MERINGUE SHARDS

1 cup aquafaba (see Note)
1¼ cups sugar
1 tsp vanilla extract
½ tsp cream of tartar

POPCORN-CHARDONNAY ICE CREAM
Heat oil in a saucepan over medium-high heat. Add popcorn kernels, cover and pop for 2 to 4 minutes, until the popping subsides. Set aside.

Bring Chardonnay to a simmer in a medium saucepan and cook for 5 minutes, or until it has reduced to ⅓ cup.

To the popcorn pan, add sugar, reduced Chardonnay, cream and milk. Bring to a simmer, cover and remove from heat immediately. Steep for 30 minutes. Strain mixture through a fine-mesh sieve, pressing on the popcorn to extract as much liquid as possible. Return liquid to a saucepan, add vanilla and salt, and bring to a simmer.

Whisk egg yolks in a stainless steel bowl. Slowly whisk in a quarter of the hot liquid to temper the yolks. Add yolk mixture to the pan of liquid and stir constantly over medium-low heat, until mixture coats the back of a spoon. (Take care not to overcook the eggs.)

Fill a large bowl with ice water. Place the pan of ice cream base in the ice bath to fully cool. Pour cooled mixture into an ice cream maker and freeze according to the manufacturer's instructions.

VEGAN MERINGUE SHARDS Preheat oven to 200°F. Line a baking sheet with parchment paper.

In a stand mixer fitted with the whisk attachment, whip aquafaba until soft peaks form. With the motor still running, slowly add sugar and whip until sugar is fully combined and stiff peaks form. Add vanilla and cream of tartar and whip until stiff glossy peaks form.

Spread meringue onto the prepared baking sheet to a ¼-inch thickness. Bake for 1 to 2 hours, until crisp and fully dehydrated. Set aside to cool, then break into shards.

NOTE Aquafaba is the drained liquid from a can of chickpeas. It is often used as a vegan egg replacer or binder, and it can be whipped into a foam.

SABLÉ BRETON

9 egg yolks

2 cups sugar

2 cups (4 sticks) butter, room temperature

4 cups flour

2 Tbsp + 2 tsp baking powder

1 tsp salt

SESAME-MISO CARAMEL

1 cup caramel sauce

1 Tbsp tahini

1 tsp miso paste

CARAMEL POPCORN

1 Tbsp vegetable oil

2 Tbsp popcorn kernels

¼ cup brown sugar

2 Tbsp butter

Pinch of sea salt

Pinch of cream of tartar

1 Tbsp glucose syrup or corn syrup

Pinch of baking soda

SABLÉ BRETON Preheat oven to 350°F. Line a baking sheet with parchment paper.

In a stand mixer fitted with the whisk attachment, combine egg yolks and sugar and whisk until tripled in volume. Add butter and whip until smooth.

In a separate bowl, combine dry ingredients and mix well. Replace the whisk attachment on the stand mixer with the paddle, then add the dry ingredients to the wet mixture and mix until fully combined. (Do not overmix.)

Transfer mixture to the prepared baking sheet, spreading it out evenly to ¼-inch thickness. Bake for 10 to 15 minutes, until golden brown. Set aside to cool, then break into pieces.

SESAME-MISO CARAMEL Whisk together all ingredients in a small bowl. Transfer to a squeeze bottle. (If not using immediately, store in the fridge and bring to room temperature prior to serving.)

CARAMEL POPCORN Preheat oven to 350°F. Line a baking sheet with parchment paper.

Heat oil in a saucepan over medium-high heat. Add popcorn kernels, cover and pop for 2 to 4 minutes, until the popping subsides. Set aside.

Combine sugar, butter, salt, cream of tartar and glucose syrup (or corn syrup) in a small saucepan and bring to a boil. Stir in baking soda, then immediately pour mixture over popcorn. Fold in until popcorn is coated.

Spread popcorn on the prepared baking sheet and bake for 20 minutes, stirring every 5 minutes. Set aside to cool. Break up caramel popcorn.

Leftover caramel popcorn can be stored at room temperature in an airtight container for a month.

ASSEMBLY Place the broken sablé in the bottom of 4 bowls. Squeeze a small pool of caramel sauce into each bowl. Top each serving with a generous portion of ice cream, then garnish with caramel popcorn and meringue shards. Serve immediately.

BNA BREWING CO. & EATERY

Justin Best
KELOWNA

In the early twentieth century, this rambling old brick building was used by the British North American Tobacco Company to dry and warehouse tobacco leaves. Today, it houses BNA Brewing Co. & Eatery, the centrepiece of Nixon Hospitality's growing food-and-drink empire.

"Nixon" is Kyle and Carolyn Nixon. The Nixon family, under the leadership of Kyle's father, Jim, owned the famous Hotel Eldorado for twenty-five years, until he sold it in 2014. Kyle managed the "El" for a decade, and it's where he met chef Justin Best, a former New Brunswicker who had cooked at high-level hotels and restaurants in Ottawa and Banff.

In 2015, when Nixon had the idea of starting a brewery in a "big old warehouse on the edge of town," Best joined him as head chef. They also transformed the former Sturgeon Hall into Skinny Duke's Glorious Emporium and Doc Willoughby's Pub into Bernie's Supper Club & Cinema. And all while Best has been cooking the beer-friendly food he loves the most.

His globetrotting menu features everything from Peruvian-style fish tacos to vegan cauliflower korma to Thai-flavoured coconut curry broth. "It was all French techniques in my mid to late twenties, but I was bored with passing purées and cooking with butter," he explains.

And he's still searching for exciting new flavours. "We go on three-day trips to seven or eight restaurants and figure out the dishes we want to try. Most everything we put on the menu at BNA comes after a food trip."

Just don't try to define Best's cuisine. "People have gotten away from classifying restaurants: this is Italian or this is Chinese," he says. "It's the same cooking principles with different ingredients. It's fusion done well, not fusion confusion."

Thai Coconut Curry Broth with Mussels and Clams

"Thai food is so interesting," says chef Justin Best. "It might have thirty-five ingredients, but everything comes together with a balance of sweet, sour, salty and spicy flavours." You can also serve the coconut curry broth on its own, as is—or, as a variation, strain the broth once cooked and add your favourite noodles. SERVES 6 TO 8

BNA Brewing
76 Wolverine Lager

COCONUT CURRY BROTH

1 to 2 Tbsp vegetable oil

1 (3-inch) piece of ginger, peeled and cut into large chunks

6 cloves garlic, chopped

3 shallots, chopped

1 long stalk lemongrass, chopped

Bunch of cilantro, leaves separated and reserved, stems chopped (divided)

1 bird's eye chili

2 lime leaves

4 pods green cardamom

1 Tbsp ground coriander

1 Tbsp curry powder

1½ tsp fennel seeds

1½ tsp ground turmeric

1 Tbsp tomato paste

1 Tbsp red curry paste, such as Mae Ploy

1 (400-mL) can coconut milk, plus extra if needed

2 cups whipping (33%) cream, plus extra if needed

1 cup white wine

1 cup clam nectar

½ cup fish sauce

2 Tbsp brown sugar, plus extra if needed

Juice of 2 limes, plus extra if needed

¼ cup (½ stick) butter

ASSEMBLY

2 lbs Salt Spring Island mussels, scrubbed and debearded

2 lbs littleneck clams, scrubbed

Bunch of green onions, sliced diagonally, for garnish

Reserved cilantro leaves, roughly chopped, for garnish

1 tomato, seeded and diced, for garnish

1 loaf French sourdough, to serve

COCONUT CURRY BROTH Heat oil in a heavy-bottomed saucepan over medium heat, until oil begins to shimmer. Add ginger and sear for 1 minute, until cara-melized. Add garlic, shallots, lemongrass, cilantro stems, chili and lime leaves. Reduce heat to medium-low and sauté for 5 to 10 minutes. (If the saucepan looks dry, add a bit more oil.)

Add cardamom, coriander, curry pow-der, fennel seeds, turmeric, tomato paste and curry paste. Stir for 3 to 4 minutes, until fragrant.

Pour in coconut milk, cream, wine, clam nectar and fish sauce. Stir in brown sugar and lime juice and simmer for 5 to 10 min-utes. Reduce heat to low, then stir in butter.

Taste the broth. If it's sweet, add the juice of half a lime. If it's too acidic, add a pinch of brown sugar. If the broth has reduced too far and is salt forward, add another ½ cup cream or half a can of coconut milk to the broth. Keep warm.

ASSEMBLY Place mussels and clams in a large bowl in the sink. Add cold water to purge the clams of sand. Transfer mussels into a clean bowl. Swish the clams around gently in the cold water, then transfer them to the bowl of mussels. Discard any broken mussels or clams.

Heat coconut curry broth over medium heat. Add mussels and clams and cover. Cook for 10 minutes, or until shells open up. Discard any unopened mussels and clams.

Ladle out broth, mussels and clams into bowls and top each with green onions, cilantro leaves and tomatoes. Serve imme-diately with crusty sourdough.

Beef Rendang

This intense Southeast Asian dish is considered by many "the king of curries." While this dry curry has relatively little sauce, it more than makes up for it in flavour. It is bursting with aromatic spices—cinnamon, cardamom and star anise—as well as fresh aromatics including lemongrass, garlic and ginger. Most of all, the beef is so tender it falls apart. "I love beef rendang," says chef Justin Best. "The rendang is money." Note that you will need to cure the beef at least four hours, then cook it for another three to four hours. SERVES 4

BNA Brewing
Otis Stout

BEEF

⅓ cup brown sugar

⅓ cup salt

4 lbs boneless beef short ribs or chuck flat, cut into large pieces

AROMATIC BASE

6 cloves garlic

4 stalks lemongrass heart, woody bits removed, chopped

3 large shallots, roughly chopped

1 (3-inch) piece ginger, peeled and chopped

3 pods green cardamom

1 star anise

⅔ cup brown sugar

1½ tsp ground cumin

1 tsp ground turmeric

1 tsp curry powder

1 tsp ground coriander

½ tsp ground cloves

½ tsp ground cinnamon

2 (400-mL) cans coconut milk

½ cup tamarind concentrate

2 Tbsp sambal oelek (Indonesian chili paste)

1 Tbsp vegetable oil

BRAISE

4 star anise

2 lime leaves

½ cinnamon stick

4 cups water

BEEF The night before you make your rendang, line a baking sheet with plastic wrap.

In a small bowl, mix sugar and salt. Place beef on the prepared baking sheet, then pat the cure over all sides of the meat. Wrap tightly in plastic wrap and refrigerate for at least 4 hours, or ideally overnight.

AROMATIC BASE Purée all ingredients in a high-speed blender on high speed. Transfer to a large bowl.

BRAISE Add all ingredients to the puréed aromatic base. Set aside.

ASSEMBLY Preheat oven to 300°F. Rinse beef under cold running water and pat dry.

Heat oil in a large Dutch oven over medium-high heat. Add beef and sear on all sides to caramelize. Pour braising mixture into pan and cover. Cook in the oven for 3 to 4 hours, until beef is fork tender and nearly falling apart. Transfer beef to a plate and set aside.

Strain the braising liquid, then discard the solids and skim as much fat off it as you can. (See Note.) Return the braising liquid to the pan. Add coconut, coconut milk, tomato paste and lime juice. Simmer over medium-low heat for 25 minutes, until reduced by two-thirds and thick enough to coat the back of a spoon. Season to taste. If it is too sour, add a pinch of brown sugar. If it's too sweet, add more lime juice or a tablespoon of tamarind concentrate.

Increase oven temperature to 375°F. Add the beef back into the sauce, cover with a lid and cook for 20 minutes until heated through. Remove from the oven.

ASSEMBLY

3 Tbsp canola oil

½ cup unsweetened
desiccated coconut

1 (400-mL) can coconut milk

⅓ cup tomato paste

Juice of 2 limes, plus extra
if needed

Pinch of brown sugar,
if needed

1 Tbsp tamarind concentrate,
if needed

TO SERVE

1 tomato, chopped

1 cup sliced green onions

5 Tbsp crushed toasted
cashews

Bunch of cilantro leaves,
roughly chopped

Unsweetened desiccated
coconut, toasted

Steamed jasmine or basmati
rice, to serve

TO SERVE Garnish with tomato, green onions, cashews, cilantro and toasted coconut. (Alternatively, place garnishes in individual condiment bowls for guests to add their own.) Serve rendang beef with steamed rice and a generous amount of sauce.

NOTE If you are not serving this right away, cool the meat in the liquid before skimming the fat and straining out the solids. This prevents it from drying out during the cooling process. The "fat cap" will also solidify at the top of the pan, making it easy to discard.

BOUCHONS BISTRO

Stéphane and Béatrice Facon

KELOWNA

Bouchons Bistro is all about *gastronomie traditionelle,* according to co-owner and chef Stéphane Facon. "It's a classic French restaurant, comprising a bistro and a brasserie. We just want to serve nice food to our guests."

Back home in France, Stéphane was a manager for the beauty brand Caudalie when a motorbike accident prompted him to change careers and follow his passion. "I returned to school and learned how to make bread and pastry," he says. In 2001, he and his wife, Béatrice, moved to Shediac, New Brunswick, where they opened a bakery café— but soon realized, "It's too small and too cold."

When a friend suggested they try Vancouver or Kelowna instead, Stéphane says, "We decided to move to Kelowna because the weather is better and there is fresh vegetables and wine. It's a very nice city."

That was 2015. A year later, they bought the twelve-year-old Bouchons (fittingly, for wine country, the name means "corks"), where he and Béatrice work happily together. "We are good team players," he says. "Our daughter Agathe has started working with us, so it's become a family business."

Everything is made from scratch, using as many local products as possible. They serve traditional fare such as cassoulet, escargot, bouillabaisse, steak (because the guests demand it) and a French hamburger topped with truffle mayo and foie gras. "Just don't ask me to put ketchup on it because I can't," Stéphane says.

In other words, Bouchons is a perfect little taste of Paris in downtown Kelowna.

Chicken Liver Mousse with Porto Jelly

This luxuriously silky spread from Bouchons owner Stéphane Facon makes a perfect appetizer for a party or a lovely addition to a charcuterie board. Serve it with crackers or sliced baguette, some cornichons on the side and a glass of juicy red. MAKES 3 CUPS

 Châteauneuf-du-Pape

CHICKEN LIVER MOUSSE

1 lb chicken livers, thawed if frozen

2 cups dry white wine

⅓ cup white wine vinegar

1 bay leaf

1 Tbsp black peppercorns

⅔ cup (1⅓ sticks) butter, room temperature

1 clove garlic

2 Tbsp brandy

⅔ cup whipping (33%) cream

Salt and black pepper, to taste

½ tsp dried thyme

PORTO JELLY

4 sheets gelatin (preferably silver)

1½ cups ruby or tawny Port

1½ Tbsp sugar

Salt and black pepper, to taste

CHICKEN LIVER MOUSSE Chill 4 individual ramekins or 125-mL Mason jars in the fridge until needed.

Rinse chicken livers in a colander under cool running water until water runs clear. Transfer to a bowl and soak in ice water for 30 minutes.

Combine wine, vinegar, bay leaf and black peppercorns in a medium saucepan and warm over medium-high heat. Drain chicken livers, then add them to the pan. Bring to a boil and cook for 10 minutes, until the internal temperature of the livers reaches 165°F. Drain and discard spices.

In a blender or food processor, combine chicken livers, butter, garlic and brandy. With the motor still running, gradually add cream and blend until smooth. Season with salt and pepper. Pour mousse into the prepared ramekins or jars, tapping gently to remove any air pockets. Sprinkle with thyme and refrigerate until cool, about 1 hour.

PORTO JELLY Soak gelatin sheets in a small bowl of cold water for 1 to 2 minutes to soften them.

In a small saucepan, combine Port and sugar and warm over medium heat. Season with salt and pepper. Add gelatin sheets and gently stir until dissolved. Evenly divide Porto jelly among ramekins, topping the mousse. Refrigerate for at least 2 hours, until set.

Classic Bouillabaisse

Fragrant with saffron and other herbs, this classic French fish soup is Bouchons owner Stéphane Facon's favourite dish. It is a staple of the port city of Marseille, where fishers used the bony Mediterranean rockfish they were unable to sell. Rockfish are less easily available to home cooks on this side of the Atlantic, so use whatever inexpensive, firm white fish you can find. SERVES 4

 Provence Rosé

SOUP BASE

⅓ cup olive oil

4 leeks, white and light green parts only, roughly chopped

2 large onions, roughly chopped

3 cloves garlic, crushed

2 fennel bulbs, roughly chopped

1 tomato, quartered

1 (5½-oz) can tomato paste

5 star anise

2 sprigs thyme

1 bay leaf

1 tsp fennel seeds

2 lbs rockfish or firm white fish, heads, tails and bones removed and reserved

2 litres water

Salt and black pepper, to taste

½ cup dry white wine

1 Tbsp saffron

¼ tsp cayenne pepper

ASSEMBLY

20 wild shrimp (16/20 count), peeled and deveined

3 lbs rockfish or other white fish, filleted, skinned and chopped into chunks

10 sea scallops

1 lb live mussels or clams, cleaned and/or debearded

Crusty bread, to serve

SOUP BASE Heat oil in a large, heavy-bottomed saucepan over medium heat. Add leeks and onions and sauté for 10 minutes, until translucent. Stir in garlic, fennel, tomatoes and tomato paste.

Combine star anise, thyme, bay leaf and fennel seeds in a cheesecloth and add to the pan. Add in rockfish, reserved fish bones and cuttings, and the water. Season with salt and pepper. Bring to a boil, then reduce heat to medium-low. Simmer, uncovered, for 30 minutes. Remove cheesecloth of spices. Using an immersion blender or a high-power blender, blend until smooth and fine (including the rockfish, bones and cuttings). Strain by using a spoon to press the soup base through a fine-mesh strainer into another saucepan, until only the solid bits remain. Discard solids.

Add wine, saffron and cayenne pepper. Bring to a boil and boil for 15 minutes. Season with salt and pepper. Keep warm.

The soup base can be prepared in advance and stored for up to 3 days in the fridge or 6 months in the freezer.

ASSEMBLY Add shrimp, fish, scallops and mussels (or clams) to the soup base. Cook for 3 to 5 minutes, until shellfish are open fully. Discard any shells that have not opened. Season to taste.

Serve with crusty bread and a rosé wine.

CANNERY BREWING

Patt Dyck and Thomas Bridson
PENTICTON

The Okanagan Valley is famous for its wineries, but it's also developing a reputation for beer, especially in Penticton—crowned in 2020 as "Canada's craft beer capital" by Lonely Planet.

Among the city's eight craft breweries is the family-owned Cannery Brewing, known for flavourful ales, sours and lagers and an ever-changing menu of shareable, beer-friendly foods.

"We brewed our first batch of beer back on April Fool's Day in 2001. It was the Naramata Nut Brown Ale, which we consider our flagship," says Patt Dyck, who co-owns the brewery with her husband, Ron, their son Ian and lead brewer Ross Thompson.

They'd been operating a restaurant in Naramata for twenty-three years when their first brewmaster, Terry Schoffer, sourced brewhouse equipment, which they moved into an old Aylmer fruit-and-vegetable cannery in Penticton.

Fifteen years later, the old cannery could no longer support the volume of beer they were producing, so they located a funky spot downtown and built their new brewery. Today, they have a busy tap room with twelve beers on tap, an outdoor beer garden and a full-on kitchen, led by chef Thomas Bridson.

"In the early days, we created meat and cheese boards that featured wonderful local products from the Okanagan. Those boards are the backbone of our menu," Patt says. "The tap room menu is fundamentally designed for sharing. We make everything ourselves."

From their new kitchen, the selections have expanded to offer salads, rotating hummus, nachos, housemade sausage rolls, ever-changing specials and intriguing sweets such as the beer-infused ice cream sandwich. "We use the best of what our area has to offer," Patt says, "and delight in the innovation created by constant change."

Preserved Lemon Hummus, p. 55

Preserved Lemon Hummus

Cannery Brewing offers a rotating hummus on the menu, and this is one of the most popular. You can enjoy it as is, or the way chef Thomas Bridson serves it: garnished with pickled red onion and cucumber, smoked paprika, sesame seeds, fresh herbs and a drizzle of good olive oil. Note that you will need to make the preserved lemons a month in advance, so use purchased ones if you plan to make this immediately. SERVES 4

Cannery Brewing
Skaha Hazy Pale Ale

PRESERVED LEMONS

4 lemons
2 cloves
2 Tbsp salt
2 tsp sugar
¼ tsp coriander seeds
¼ tsp fennel seeds
Pinch of crushed red pepper
Sprig of thyme

PRESERVED LEMON HUMMUS

8 pieces Preserved Lemons (see here)
¼ cup Preserved Lemon brine (see here)
2 Tbsp tahini
¼ cup roasted garlic cloves
¼ cup olive oil, plus extra if needed
1 (20-oz) can chickpeas, drained and rinsed
Salt and black pepper, to taste
Juice of 1 lemon (optional)
Pita bread, crackers and/or vegetables, to serve

PRESERVED LEMONS Trim ends from the lemons, cut into quarters and squeeze out all the juice into a non-reactive bowl. Add the juiced lemon wedges to the bowl.

Combine remaining ingredients in a separate bowl and mix well. Add to the bowl of lemon wedges and toss until lemons are generously coated. Transfer mixture to a 1-litre Mason jar and top with just enough filtered water to submerge lemons. Cover with lid and set aside for three days at room temperature, occasionally turning the jar upside down and back.

Place jar in the fridge and preserve for 1 month before use. Will keep for 3 to 6 months.

PRESERVED LEMON HUMMUS Using a sharp paring knife, separate lemon rinds from pulp. Discard pulp, then set aside rinds.

Combine lemon brine and tahini in a food processor and process for a minute. (Creaming the lemon brine and tahini together first helps to create a smoother hummus.) Add lemon rinds, roasted garlic and oil and mix until smooth. Add chickpeas and process until creamy and smooth. If needed, add a little more oil to smooth it out. Season with salt and pepper. If you prefer a more citrusy hummus, add fresh lemon juice. Serve with pita bread, crackers, veggies or your favourite dipping snacks.

Potato, Camembert and Duck Pierogi

Cannery Brewing
LakeBoat
German-Style Lager

This richly flavoured dish is served at Cannery Brewing with apple relish, an orange–red currant sour cream, crispy duck skin and fried onions, but you can keep it simple with plain sour cream and it will still be delicious. MAKES 2 DOZEN PIEROGI

DUCK CONFIT

4 duck legs

2 bay leaves, crushed

2 Tbsp salt

Zest of ½ orange

2 to 3 cups melted duck fat

PIEROGI FILLING

3 bay leaves

1 shallot, roughly chopped

½ Tbsp salt, plus extra
  to taste

1 tsp black peppercorns

8 russet potatoes, peeled
  and roughly chopped

2½ Tbsp butter (divided)

¼ tsp white pepper

¼ tsp cayenne pepper

½ cup milk

Black pepper, to taste

1 cup Duck Confit (see here)

1 tsp dried thyme

½ tsp ground clove

DUCK CONFIT In a large non-reactive bowl, combine duck legs, bay leaves, salt and orange zest. Cover and refrigerate overnight or up to 24 hours to cure.

Preheat oven to 200°F.

Rinse legs under cold running water, then pat dry. Place duck legs in a deep 9-inch casserole dish and cover with enough duck fat to submerge completely.

Cover with a heatproof lid or aluminum foil and cook in the oven for 6 to 8 hours, until duck is tender and almost falling apart. Using a slotted spoon or tongs, carefully transfer the cooked duck legs to a chopping board and set aside to cool.

Gently remove the skin and reserve. (It can be crisped up for a tasty, crunchy garnish.) Pull meat from bones and shred. Set aside. The duck fat can be strained and refrigerated or frozen for your next batch of confit.

NOTE You will have more duck confit than required for this recipe. You can freeze the extra meat for another time, add more to the filling for a meatier pierogi or sprinkle it over the finished dish.

PIEROGI FILLING Fill a medium saucepan with water. Add bay leaves, shallots, salt and peppercorns and bring to a boil over high heat. Add potatoes, then reduce heat to medium. Simmer for 15 minutes, until potatoes have softened. Drain, then discard peppercorns and bay leaves.

Transfer cooked potatoes to a stand mixer fitted with a paddle attachment or to a mixing bowl. Add 2 tablespoons butter, white pepper, cayenne pepper and milk. Mash until light, smooth and creamy. Season to taste with salt and black pepper.

In a separate bowl, combine duck confit, thyme, clove and the remaining ½ tablespoon of butter. Fold the duck mixture into the potatoes. Season with salt and black pepper. Set aside.

PIEROGI DOUGH

3 cups flour

1 tsp salt

¾ cup water

2 Tbsp butter

ASSEMBLY

Pierogi Dough (see here)

Flour, for dusting

Pierogi Filling (see here)

1 wheel Camembert
 (preferably Poplar Grove),
 sectioned into 24 pieces

1 to 2 Tbsp butter

Salt and black pepper,
 to taste

Fried onions, sausage,
 Duck Confit (see here)
 or crispy duck skin,
 for garnish (optional)

Sour cream, for garnish
 (optional)

PIEROGI DOUGH Combine flour and salt in a large mixing bowl.

Place water and butter in a small saucepan and gently simmer until the temperature reaches 175°F to 195°F. Pour into dry ingredients and mix until roughly combined.

Using your hands, or in a stand mixer fitted with a dough hook, knead dough for 5 minutes, until smooth and elastic. If mixture is dry, add a little water, a teaspoon at a time, and knead until it is the desired consistency. Wrap dough tightly in plastic wrap and allow to rest at room temperature for 30 minutes.

ASSEMBLY Divide dough into quarters and wrap all unused portions in plastic wrap until needed. Turn a piece of dough onto a lightly floured surface and roll out to a ⅛-inch thickness. If the dough is too difficult to roll out, let it rest for another 10 minutes.

Using a 3-inch ring mould or paring knife, cut rounds out of dough. Gather any scraps, then knead them together and cover with plastic wrap. Rest for a few minutes, then roll and cut them. Repeat with remaining dough. Makes 24 rounds.

Place a tablespoon of filling on each round. Add a piece of Camembert, then fold dough over to create a semi-circle. Press edges together, sealing and crimping with your fingers. Do not leave any gaps or the pierogi will burst open during blanching. Place on a floured baking sheet. Cover loosely with a cloth. Repeat with the remaining pierogi, evenly spacing them apart on the baking sheet. (To freeze, place the sheet of pierogi in the freezer for 2 to 3 hours. Transfer to a zip-top bag and freeze for up to 3 months.)

Bring a large saucepan of water to a simmer. Working in small batches, lower pierogi into the boiling water and gently stir them to prevent them from sticking to the bottom or to each other. Cook for 5 minutes, or until they float to the surface. Using a slotted spoon, transfer to a plate. Repeat with the remaining pierogi.

Heat butter in a frying pan over medium heat. Working in batches, add pierogi and pan-fry for 5 minutes, turning once or twice, until they form a golden-brown crust. Transfer to a serving plate.

Top with fried onions, sausage, duck confit, duck skin and/or a dollop of sour cream (if using). Serve.

CHAOS BISTRO AT EX NIHILO VINEYARDS

Nina Harder and Danny Tipper
LAKE COUNTRY

It began with a work of art. In 1999, founders Decoa and Jeff Harder were in San Francisco when they came across a working model for *Ex Nihilo*, a sculpture created by the artist Frederick Hart for the Washington National Cathedral. Awed by the power of the work, whose name means "out of nothing," Jeff proclaimed that one day they would build a winery and call it Ex Nihilo.

Four years later, they found a perfect ten-acre property on a hill in Lake Country and, out of almost nothing, Ex Nihilo Vineyards was born. In 2018, wine lovers Janet and Mike Azhadi joined the Ex Nihilo team as principle proprietors and began elevating the Ex Nihilo experience. In 2023, Janet and Mike Azhadi became sole proprietors, and today this family-run boutique winery produces a wide range of award-winning wines and is also home to Chaos Bistro—Chaos, in ancient Greece, being the primeval emptiness, the "nihilo" from which the world was wrought. It's also where

chef Danny Tipper makes his bright, fresh, ingredient-driven cuisine.

Tipper, who joined Chaos in 2021, was born and raised in the Okanagan, as was Nina Harder, the couple's daughter, who is the winery's marketing co-ordinator and brand ambassador. "We have a fairly small team, but we have two kitchens here, an outdoor kitchen with a forno oven and an indoor prep kitchen," he says. He uses the oven mainly for gourmet pizzas topped with fresh produce, much of it from the farmer next door.

Lately, Tipper has been spending more time in the cellar with winemaker Jim Faulkner, training his palate and his skill at pairing food with wine. "It's inspiring writing menus and working kind of backwards," he says, adding, "The menu is focused on local. It's a natural here. We have it all." And that's definitely not nothing.

Green Apple and Riesling BBQ Sauce

At Chaos Bistro, the best dishes come out of the wood-burning outdoor oven, and this versatile sauce brings them to life. "The sauce works great on grilled chicken or ribs as it can reduce on the meat and get nice and sticky. It is also perfect as a condiment on grilled burgers," says chef Danny Tipper. SERVES 4

 Ex Nihilo Riesling

1 Tbsp extra-virgin olive oil

4 shallots, thinly sliced

2 large Granny Smith apples, unpeeled, cored and finely chopped

1 Tbsp salt, plus extra to taste

½ tsp black pepper, plus extra to taste

1 cup Ex Nihilo Riesling

1 cup brown sugar

1 tsp white miso paste

½ tsp garlic powder

Pinch of crushed red pepper (optional)

¼ cup sherry vinegar or red wine vinegar

1 Tbsp lemon juice

1 Tbsp molasses

Heat oil in a heavy-bottomed saucepan over medium heat. Add shallots, apples, salt and black pepper and sauté for 5 minutes, until caramelized. Deglaze with Riesling and cook for another 5 minutes, until reduced by half.

Add remaining ingredients and mix well. Simmer for 20 minutes, or until sauce has thickened and liquid is reduced by half. Remove from heat.

Using an immersion blender, blend sauce to your desired consistency. Set aside to cool. Season to taste with salt and black pepper.

Sauce can be stored in an airtight container or sauce bottle in the fridge for 2 weeks.

Cabernet Franc-Braised Short Ribs

This hearty braised beef dish uses what is fast becoming one of the Okanagan Valley's—and Ex Nihilo's—signature grape varieties, Cabernet Franc. This is an ideal dish to make ahead for a dinner party. The flavours simply become deeper and better integrated with time. SERVES 4

Ex Nihilo XXX
Cabernet Franc

SHORT RIBS

4½ lbs bone-in beef
   short ribs or boneless
   chuck flat
4 cloves
2 star anise
2 pods black cardamom
2 Tbsp black peppercorns
2 Tbsp fennel seeds
2 Tbsp dried thyme
3 Tbsp salt

BRAISE

4 large tomatoes, chopped
   (4 cups)
½ cup brown sugar
1 (750-mL) bottle Ex Nihilo
   Cabernet Franc
¼ cup molasses
2 Tbsp tomato paste
2 Tbsp soy sauce
2 to 3 Tbsp vegetable oil
5 shallots, thinly sliced
10 cloves garlic, finely
   chopped
10 cremini mushrooms,
   thinly sliced
6 cups beef stock
1 cinnamon stick
Fresh pasta, to serve
Seasonal vegetables,
   steamed or grilled,
   to serve

SHORT RIBS Clean short ribs and remove excess fat and membrane from the back side. Set aside.

Add all spices, except for salt, to a small frying pan and toast over medium heat, until fragrant. Set aside to cool slightly. Using a mortar and pestle or spice grinder, grind the spices. Transfer to a small bowl and stir in salt.

Rub seasoning over short ribs and allow to marinate in the fridge for 2 to 12 hours.

BRAISE Preheat oven to 325°F.

In a non-reactive bowl, combine tomatoes, brown sugar, wine (reserving ¼ cup to deglaze pan), molasses, tomato paste and soy sauce. Set aside.

Add enough oil to coat the bottom of a large, heavy-bottomed ovenproof saucepan or Dutch oven and heat over medium-high heat. Working in batches if necessary, add short ribs and sear on all sides. Transfer to a plate and set aside.

Add shallots, garlic and mushrooms to the saucepan and cook for 10 minutes until caramelized. Deglaze with the reserved wine, then stir in tomato mixture. Simmer for 15 minutes, until reduced by a third. Add stock and cinnamon stick.

Return short ribs back to the pan and bring to a gentle simmer. Cover and braise in the oven for 3 to 3½ hours, turning the ribs every hour, until very tender.

Discard cinnamon sick. Transfer short ribs to a plate. Using an immersion blender, blend sauce to your desired consistency. Return short ribs to pan.

Serve with sauce over fresh pasta, with vegetables.

COCCARO GROUP

Luigi and Lauretta Coccaro
KELOWNA

The Italian word *bussola* means "compass" and, in the early 1970s, the needle was pointing due west for Franco Coccaro and his business partner. They travelled across Canada until they discovered a beautiful city by the lake. Kelowna, they decided, would be a good place to live and work. And, in 1974, they opened La Bussola, Kelowna's first Italian fine-dining experience.

By 1990, Franco's wife Lauretta was head chef and co-owner, serving up finely crafted classic Italian fare like veal piccata and eggplant parmigiana and adding a few innovative twists of her own. Their children, Ersilia and Luigi, grew up in the family business, and in 2000, Luigi decided to make it his career.

But rather than cooking, Luigi focused on wine instead. ("I always wanted to be in the kitchen, but they didn't want me," he says.) He earned his Wine & Spirit Education Trust (WSET) diploma at the age of twenty-seven and brought sophisticated depth to the wine cellar at La Bussola. He's since expanded the business, opening the casual Curious Café in 2014, followed by the Bar Norcino speakeasy in 2016 and the Korean-Italian Gather in 2018. In 2021, he launched Franco's Liquor Store, which specializes in online sales of fine wines and spirits.

"Growing up in a restaurant was fun, but you don't realize how much work it is until you do it yourself. And working with family is entertaining, too," Luigi says with a laugh, adding, "Growing up, we would all cook together. We would always have Sunday dinner at mom's house. Everything she does is in her head or, if it's written down, it's in Italian. Me and mom love cooking together."

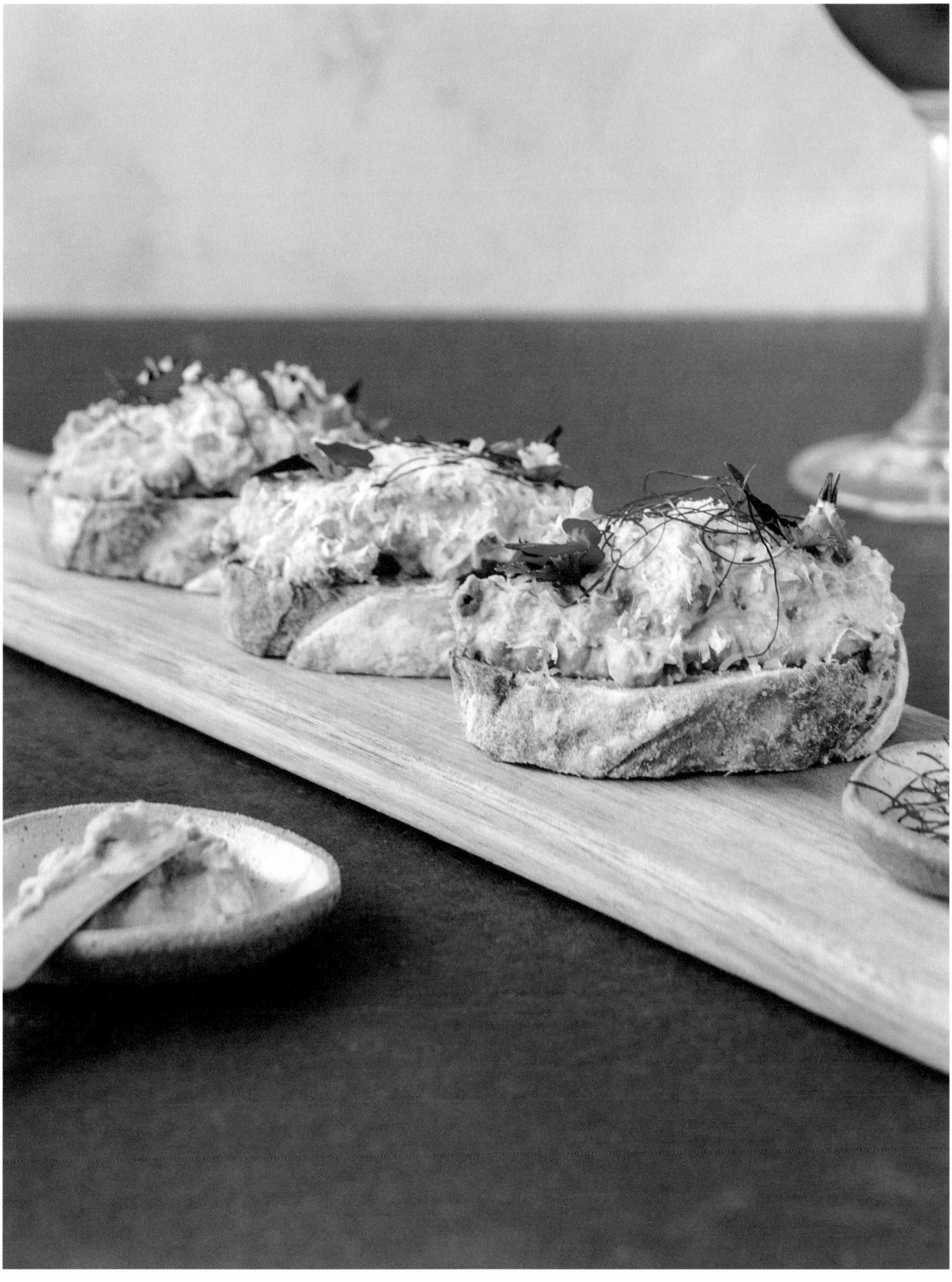

Snap Pea Bruschetta, p. 64

Snap Pea Bruschetta

What a lovely and simple snack this is from the Coccaro Group's La Bussola restaurant. Like the best Italian recipes, it uses fresh, quality ingredients—in this case, spring peas, pecorino and good olive oil—to create something transcendent. And it pairs beautifully with herbal white wines like Grüner Veltliner—or with the Coccaro Group's Summer Spritz (page 65). Although the recipe suggests toasting the bread under the broiler, it would also be delicious grilled over charcoal. SERVES 4 TO 6

Grüner Veltliner

5 cups shelled fresh snap peas or frozen peas, defrosted

½ cup extra-virgin olive oil (divided)

Juice of 2 lemons

4 cloves garlic (divided)

¼ cup pecorino, plus extra for garnish

1 Tbsp thinly sliced mint

¼ to ½ tsp crushed red pepper, to taste

Grated zest of 1 lemon

Salt and black pepper, to taste

1 loaf sourdough bread, cut into ¾-inch-thick slices

Edible flowers, for garnish (optional)

Preheat oven to 400°F. Line a baking sheet with parchment paper.

Spread peas evenly over the prepared baking sheet. Drizzle with 1 to 2 tablespoons olive oil. Bake for 10 minutes. Set aside to cool.

In a blender or food processor, combine half the cooked peas (about 2½ cups), ¼ cup oil and lemon juice and blend until smooth. Transfer to a large bowl.

Finely chop 3 cloves of garlic. Add to the bowl, along with the remaining peas and the pecorino, mint, crushed red pepper, lemon zest, salt and black pepper. Mix thoroughly, while crushing and smashing peas. Season to taste.

Turn oven to broil. Cut the remaining clove of garlic in half. Toast bread slices on both sides, rub with garlic and drizzle with oil. Put in oven and toast again.

Spread the smashed pea mixture over the bread. Grate a generous amount of pecorino overtop, sprinkle with more black pepper, garnish with edible flowers (if using) and serve.

Summer Spritz

Could anything be more refreshing than the bittersweet flavours and gentle bubbles of a summery spritz? This version from the Coccaro Group's restaurant Gather (and new liquor store) uses Hotel Starlino Rosé Aperitivo, a pretty pink aperitivo made with grapefruit and lemon peel, and tops it with Empress 1908 Gin, whose purple hue transforms to pink when it comes in contact with citrus. Beautiful. SERVES 1

2 oz Hotel Starlino Rosé Aperitivo

2 oz Prosecco

Club soda

Blackberries

¼ oz Empress 1908 Gin

Edible flowers, for garnish (optional)

Fill a large wine glass with ice. Add rosé aperitivo, then top with Prosecco, club soda and blackberries. Gently float gin on top. Garnish with edible flowers (if using).

DEEP ROOTS WINERY

Will Hardman and Chris Van Hooydonk

NARAMATA

At this family-owned and -operated winery on the Naramata Bench, the roots really do run deep. "I'm fourth generation and my baby boy is now the fifth generation on this farm," explains winemaker Will Hardman. "That's where the Deep Roots name comes from. We just celebrated our centennial."

His dad, Bryan Hardman, took over the farm from his own father in 1971. Back then, they were growing cherries, pears, apricots and apples. In the 1990s, he bought a second property in Naramata to plant some vines, and sold his grapes to local wineries for the next decade. "My dad was part of the first wave of people replanting grapes on the bench," Will says. Eventually they replanted the original property and, in 2012, made their first vintage. In 2014, they opened the tasting room, and they've never looked back.

Will joined the business in 2003. "I came back from university with no idea what I wanted to do and started working for my dad," he says. He spent time working in New Zealand and South Africa and returned to the Okanagan raring to grow and build the winery.

Deep Roots is best known for its reds, especially Gamay and Syrah—the Syrah was named B.C. Lieutenant Governor's Awards Wine of the Year in 2019—and everything is estate grown. Most of all, Deep Roots is all about family. Everyone pitches in—Bryan as proprietor and grower; mom Deb overseeing the tasting room; Will's partner Heather doing the bookkeeping and managing the wine club; sister Erika helping out in the tasting room on summer breaks and his other sister, Marlis Yassin, shares her accounting expertise as a business resource for the winery. Smokey and Kenya, the winery dogs, are the friendly welcoming committee.

After all, as Will says, "When you have wine business in the family, people want to be a part of it."

Chef Chris Van Hooydonk, who has created two delicious recipes to pair with the wines, is the proprietor of Backyard Farm and a passionate believer in the importance of growing food.

Chocolate Pot de Crème with Wine-Spiced Cherries

Here, Backyard Farm chef Chris Van Hooydonk pairs a creamy chocolate dessert with Deep Roots Winery's Syrah. "This recipe brings forth the chocolate and dark fruit notes of a Syrah. Often, we will suggest a dessert pairing with a Syrah as a finish to a multi-course meal. The custard base coats the palate, allowing nuances of the wine to shine through." SERVES 4 TO 6

Deep Roots
Winery Syrah

WINE-SPICED CHERRIES

½ cup sugar

2 Tbsp water

½ cup red wine (preferably Deep Roots Winery Syrah)

2 cups frozen pitted cherries

1 cinnamon stick

CHOCOLATE POT DE CRÈME

½ cup good-quality dark chocolate callets or chips

¼ cup sugar

Small pinch of sea salt

1¼ cups heavy (36%) cream

3 farm-fresh egg yolks

½ tsp vanilla extract

½ tsp cocoa powder

ASSEMBLY

Wine-Spiced Cherries (see here)

Mint leaves, for garnish

Coffee meringue, chocolate or shortbread, to serve (optional)

WINE-SPICED CHERRIES Combine sugar and water in a medium saucepan and bring to a simmer over medium-high heat. Cook for 5 to 10 minutes until sugar caramelizes and turns amber.

Quickly pour in wine and stir to dissolve the caramel. Add cherries and cinnamon stick. Simmer on medium heat for 5 minutes, just until cherries are cooked through and slightly soft.

Strain cherry liquid through a fine-mesh sieve into a small saucepan and simmer for 15 to 20 minutes over medium heat, until syrupy. (Reserve cherries.) Set aside to cool to room temperature and stir in cherries. Set aside until needed.

CHOCOLATE POT DE CRÈME Preheat oven to 300°F. Arrange 6 (250-mL) wide-mouth Mason jars or ramekins in a roasting pan.

Combine chocolate, sugar and salt in a mixing bowl. In a small saucepan, scald cream over medium heat, until just steaming but not boiling. Pour hot cream over chocolate and whisk until smooth. Set aside to cool slightly.

In a separate bowl, combine yolks, vanilla and cocoa powder. Working very slowly, and whisking constantly, gradually pour warm chocolate-cream mixture into egg mixture. (Working slowly tempers the eggs and prevents them scrambling.) Strain mixture through a fine-mesh sieve.

Pour into Mason jars (or ramekins), filling them halfway. Add warm water to the roasting pan until it reaches halfway up the outsides of the jars. Cover pan with aluminum foil and bake for 30 minutes, or until set. The pots de crème should be slightly jiggly, but not liquid. Remove and set aside to cool for at least 2 hours.

ASSEMBLY Top each chilled pot de crème with a few wine-spiced cherries. Garnish with a mint leaf and serve with coffee meringue, chocolate or shortbread (if using).

Charred Apple and Triple Cream Brie Tart, Pumpkin Seed Butter, Apricot Gastrique

Backyard Farm chef Chris Van Hooydonk has paired this appetizer recipe with the popular Deep Roots Sauvignon Blanc. "As this varietal tends to have higher acidity, this recipe helps to bring forth nuances of fruit with the apple contribution, and the fat from the brie component coats the palate, bringing forward underlying flavour profiles," he says. SERVES 4

Deep Roots Winery
Sauvignon Blanc

APRICOT GASTRIQUE

2 Tbsp olive oil

1 shallot, finely chopped

6 to 8 apricots, pitted and halved (2 cups)

3 Tbsp honey

3 Tbsp rice wine vinegar or white wine vinegar

¼ tsp sea salt

PUMPKIN SEED BUTTER

1 cup shelled pumpkin seeds

½ tsp sea salt

1 to 2 tsp grapeseed oil

1 tsp honey

CHARRED APPLE AND TRIPLE CREAM BRIE TART

1 sheet full-butter puff pastry

4 apples, such as Ambrosia, Red Delicious or Gala, unpeeled, cored and cut horizontally into ½-inch rounds (you should have 3 rounds per person/tart)

Olive oil, as needed

Sea salt, to taste

1 small wheel triple-cream brie

Basil or sage leaves, sliced, plus extra for garnish

Pumpkin Seed Butter (see here)

Apricot Gastrique (see here)

Reserved toasted pumpkin seeds (see here) or fresh pomegranate seeds, for garnish (optional)

APRICOT GASTRIQUE Heat oil in a saucepan over medium heat. Add shallots and sauté for 3 to 5 minutes, or until translucent. Add apricots, honey, vinegar and salt, then reduce heat to low. Cook for 15 minutes, or until fruit is macerated. Set aside to cool.

Transfer to a blender and purée until smooth. Refrigerate until needed.

PUMPKIN SEED BUTTER Preheat oven to 300°F.

Arrange pumpkin seeds on a baking sheet and toast for 15 minutes, tossing frequently, until fragrant and slightly golden. Set aside to cool slightly. Reserve 1 teaspoon pumpkin seeds for a garnish.

Combine remaining pumpkin seeds, salt, oil and honey in a food processor. Blend until smooth, scraping sides down often. Set aside until needed.

CHARRED APPLE AND TRIPLE CREAM BRIE TART Preheat oven to 375°F. Line a baking sheet with parchment paper.

Roll out puff pastry dough to a ¼-inch thickness and cut out 4 (4-inch) circles. Arrange the pastry rounds on the prepared baking sheet. Cover them with a second sheet of parchment and another baking sheet. Bake pastry rounds, pressed between the two baking sheets, for 10 minutes, or until golden brown. Set aside to cool.

Preheat a grill over medium-high heat. Brush sliced apple rounds with oil and season lightly with salt. Grill for 3 minutes per side, until they have grill marks. Set aside to cool.

Preheat oven to 300°F. Line a baking sheet with parchment paper.

Section brie into 8 (½-inch) slices. To each pastry base, add an apple round, a slice of brie and a scattering of basil (or sage) leaves. Repeat the 3 layers once more and top with remaining apple round. Warm tarts in the oven for 6 to 8 minutes, until brie starts to melt.

ASSEMBLY Spread a small amount of pumpkin seed butter on a plate. Spoon apricot gastrique around it (as a sauce). Place warm tart in centre and garnish with pumpkin or pomegranate seeds (if using). Top with basil (or sage) leaves.

EL TAQUERO

Israel Camarillo

KELOWNA

When Israel Camarillo—known to all as Izzy—moved to Vancouver from Mexico City back in 2009, he started making his favourite tacos for his "gringo" friends on periodic taco nights. By 2014, as many as forty people would show up for his taco nights. "Those parties were so amazing. It was a lot of music, good food and fun," he recalls.

In 2015, Izzy and his partner Marnie Burnett moved to Kelowna to raise their daughter and opened El Taquero, which translates to "the taco maker." "At the time, there was very little representation of Mexican cuisine in the valley, and we were excited to share Mexican street food with a new community," Camarillo says. "We were doing this anyway, so why not do it every day?"

Now El Taquero serves more than a dozen street-style tacos, including the popular chicken tinga and beef birria, as well as cocktails (Burnett is the head Margarita shaker). The menu also includes other popular favourites like burritos, nachos and chilaquiles, a favourite on the weekend breakfast menu.

They use as much locally grown produce as they can, including serrano chilies and tomatillos. "We bring in a lot of [traditional] ingredients from back home, but there are many opportunities to work with local ingredients as well," he says. "The freshness is unparalleled."

The downtown taco shop has grown to offer catering options and private dinners to residents and visitors alike. "I love stepping into someone else's kitchen and sharing my experiences with their guests. Or serving up tacos at wedding receptions. The parties here end much earlier than back in Mexico though," Camarillo says with a laugh.

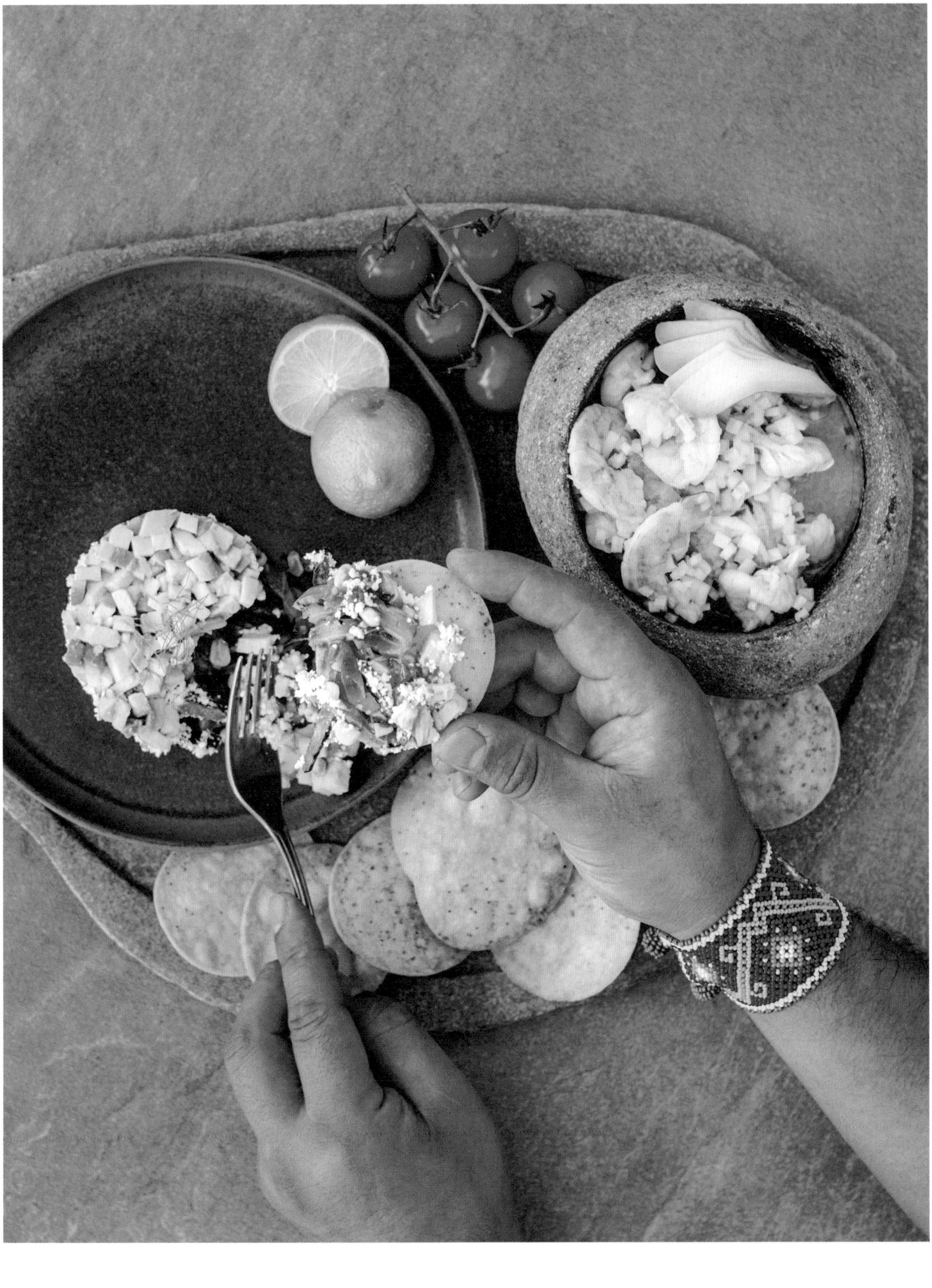

Cactus Salad, p. 73 and Aguachile, p.72

Aguachile

Aguachile is a traditional seafood ceviche from western Mexico. Chef Israel Camarillo, being based in the Okanagan, adds the local flavour of nectarines. This is a refreshing and simple dish ideal for sharing with your amigos alongside margaritas and Mexican beers. SERVES 2 TO 4

 Mexican Beer

½ lb uncooked prawns, peeled and deveined

1 nectarine, finely chopped

½ red onion, finely chopped

½ cucumber, finely chopped

½ jicama, finely chopped

4 to 8 serrano chilies, stemmed and seeded (see Note), plus extra if needed

3 cloves garlic

¼ bunch cilantro, plus extra for garnish

2 tsp dried oregano (preferably Mexican)

1 tsp ground allspice

½ tsp fine sea salt, plus extra if needed

½ tsp black pepper, plus extra if needed

½ cup lime juice

½ cup white vinegar

Tostadas or tortilla chips, to serve

Thinly slice prawns lengthwise. Keep chilled.

In a large, non-reactive mixing bowl, combine nectarine, red onions, cucumbers and jicama and mix well.

To make the marinade, combine the remaining ingredients, except the tostadas, in a blender and blend until smooth. Strain through a fine-mesh sieve. Season to taste with more chilies, salt and/or pepper.

Add prawns and marinade to the bowl of vegetables and gently toss. Cover and refrigerate for 30 minutes. The acids in the marinade will "cook" the raw prawns.

Garnish with cilantro, then serve with tostadas (or tortilla chips).

NOTE Adjust the number of chilies to your desired heat.

Cactus Salad (Ensalada de Nopales)

Nopal is the Mexican name for the pads of a specific type of cactus that is widely used in appetizers, side dishes and mains. The cactus is also known further north as prickly pear cactus, for its fruit. This traditional salad from chef Israel Camarillo is aromatic, nutritious and (relatively) easy to make, as long as you can find the ingredients. Enjoy this salad on its own or as a topping for tostadas. SERVES 4

Mexican Beer

5 cactus paddles (nopales), about 1 lb (see Note)

3 Tbsp canola oil

2 cloves garlic, finely chopped

2 ears of corn, shucked

1 lb cherry tomatoes, halved

1 Tbsp mezcal

2 serrano chilies, stemmed, seeded and finely chopped

½ white or red onion, thinly sliced

½ tsp salt

½ tsp pepper

2 avocados

Fronds of 1 fennel bulb, finely chopped

¼ bunch cilantro, leaves only

½ cup queso fresco or feta cheese

Preheat a barbecue grill over high heat. (Alternatively, preheat a broiler.)

Carefully hold a cactus paddle by its stem with kitchen tongs or a kitchen towel and using a sharp knife, trim the edges off. With the tip of the knife, scrape off the thorns. Flip over and scrape down stem until you get to the soft part. Rinse under cold running water. Repeat with the remaining nopales.

Char nopales on each side for 3 minutes, until lightly charred. Set aside until cool enough to handle. Slice the nopales into strips, then cut the strips into 3-inch segments.

Heat oil in a frying pan over medium-high heat. Add garlic and sauté for 10 seconds. Stir in corn and sauté for another 45 seconds. Add tomatoes, then pour in mezcal to create a flame. Flambé until tomatoes begin to soften.

Add chilies, onions, salt and pepper and toss vigorously. Add nopales and heat through. Transfer to a serving bowl, then let cool to room temperature.

Chop avocados, add to the bowl and toss gently. Top with fennel fronds, cilantro and queso fresco (or feta).

NOTE You can find fresh nopales or jars of chopped, cooked nopales in Mexican groceries, specialty shops and some large supermarkets.

FRANKIE WE SALUTE YOU!

Christina and Brian Skinner
KELOWNA

Frankie was a real person—in fact, there were two of them. Both Brian and Christina Skinner had grandfathers who were not only named Frank but had a great passion for growing food. "It was a no-brainer to pay homage to them and their families with this concept," says Brian, the executive chef, who insists he is "just trying to honour Christina's vision of the restaurant."

Their concept was to serve simple, wholesome, plant-forward food. "Our entire core menu is plant-based: no eggs, no dairy, no honey. Then we add eggs for brunch on the weekends," Brian says. "Three-quarters of the clientele are not vegetarian. They are just out for good food. We want to be inclusive to everybody and not be that weird vegetarian place."

Brian spent time bouncing around Michelin-starred kitchens in Europe before returning to Vancouver to open The Acorn, considered one of the world's finest plant-based restaurants. "I always wanted to do a vegetarian restaurant," he says. "Prior to that, there was no vegetarian haute cuisine—at least, not in Canada."

But then the Skinners had a baby, the Okanagan beckoned and, in 2019, they opened Frankie We Salute You!

The food here is deceptively casual, with popular dishes like chickpea fries, ranchero bowls and a vegan cauliflower queso that took Brian fourteen attempts to perfect. Guests will also find terrific cocktails and a cheerfully minimalist room designed by Christina.

What they won't find? A gigantic chef's ego.

"The fine-dining world is an extension of the chef's ego. If you take away the ego, you just have the food," he says. "This is the food people want to eat."

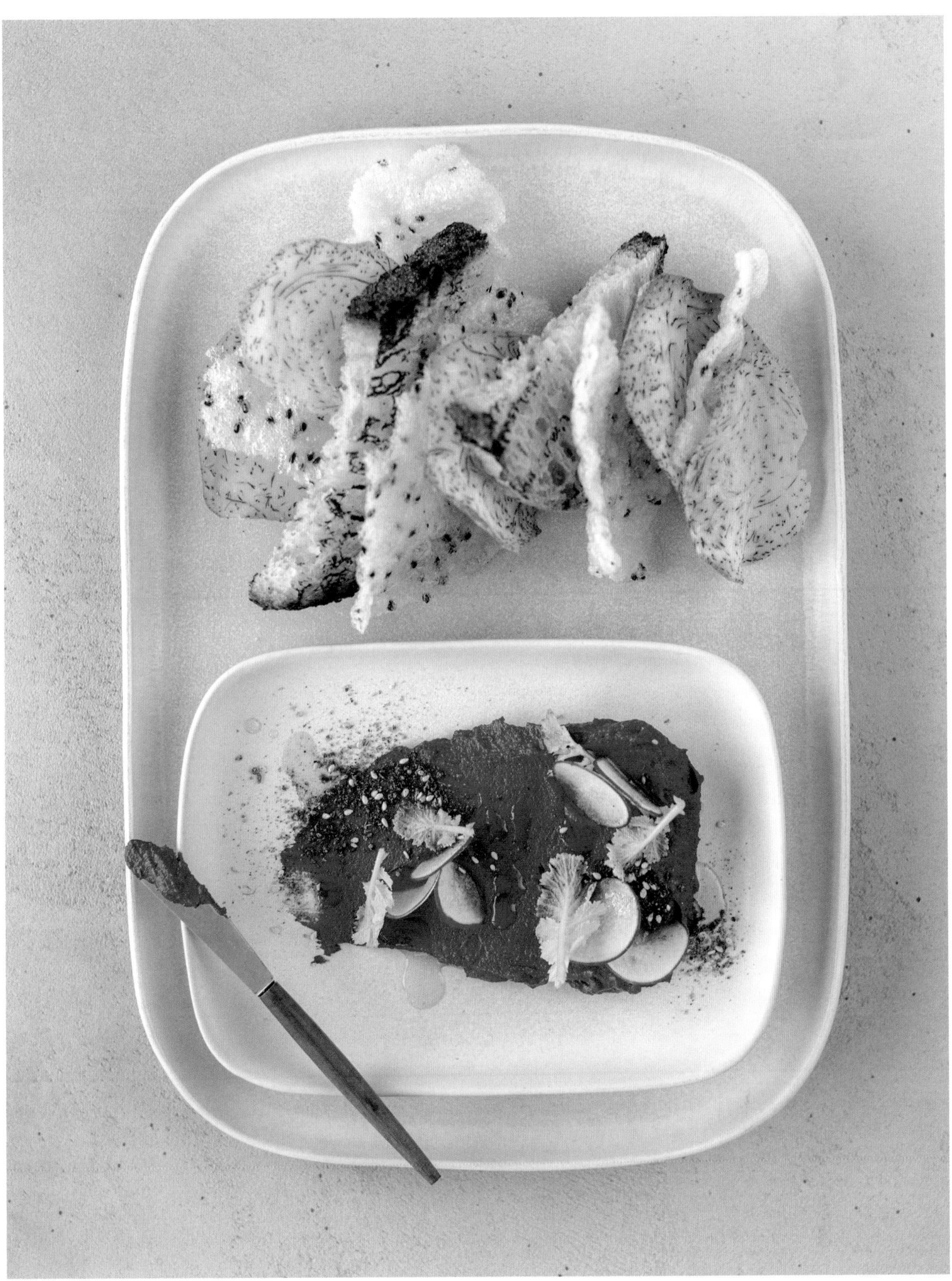

Roasted Beet Baba Ghanoush, p. 76

Roasted Beet Baba Ghanoush

Baba ghanoush is a Levantine appetizer typically made with eggplants roasted over an open flame. Here, the smoky eggplant is mixed with beets, which add a sweet earthiness as well as a pretty pink hue. Instructions have been provided for roasting eggplant in the oven, but you can do as the team at Frankie We Salute You! does and grill the eggplant over charcoal. Simply score the eggplant and grill it on each side until it's charred. No matter what, it makes the perfect addition for a backyard party. MAKES ABOUT 3 CUPS

 Spearhead Saddle Block Pinot Noir

4 medium beets

2 Tbsp canola oil

1 Italian eggplant

3 cloves garlic, finely chopped

1½ cups canned chickpeas, drained and rinsed (see Note)

3 Tbsp coconut sugar

2 Tbsp salt, plus extra if needed

1 tsp ground fennel seeds

1 tsp ground coriander

1 tsp ground cumin

¾ cup tahini

½ cup lemon juice, plus extra if needed

¼ cup olive oil, plus extra for garnish

Grated zest of 2 lemons

Sliced radish, dukkah spice blend or greens, for garnish (optional)

Crackers, pita bread or veggies crudité, to serve

Preheat oven to 375°F. Line 2 baking sheets with parchment paper.

Peel beets in the sink under running water to avoid staining your fingers. Thinly slice to ⅛-inch thickness. Put in a bowl, add canola oil and toss to coat. Spread beets on one of the prepared baking sheets and cover with another layer of parchment paper. (This allows the sugars to caramelize and also provides steam for even cooking.) Roast for 30 minutes, or until fork tender.

Using a knife, poke holes all over the eggplant. Place it on the other prepared baking sheet. Roast for 30 to 40 minutes, until browned, slightly wrinkled on the outside and tender on the inside. (A little char on the outside is OK, it's the inside flesh we want.) Set aside to cool for 5 minutes. Cut it in half and scoop out the flesh. Discard peels.

In a food processor, combine eggplant, beets and the remaining ingredients, except the crackers. Blend until smooth. Season to taste with more lemon juice or salt. Garnish with sliced radish, dukkah spice blend, greens or a drizzle of olive oil (if using). Serve with crackers, pita bread or veggies crudité on a platter.

Leftover baba ghanoush can be stored in an airtight container in the fridge for 7 days or in the freezer for up to 1 month.

NOTE Be sure to save the liquid from the canned chickpeas. Known as aquafaba, it is a delicacy in the vegan cooking world. You will need this to make the Okanagan Haskap Sour (page 77).

Okanagan Haskap Sour

Christina Skinner loves cocktails and is determined to make Frankie We Salute You! one of the Okanagan Valley's prime cocktail destinations. She uses as many local products as she can, including whisky and liqueurs from Okanagan Spirits, B.C.'s original craft distillery. The aquafaba works as egg whites do in sour cocktails but keeps this drink vegan. SERVES 1

SIMPLE SYRUP

1 cup sugar

1 cup water

OKANAGAN HASKAP SOUR

1½ oz Okanagan Spirits BRBN

1 oz lemon juice

½ oz Okanagan Spirits Haskap Liqueur

½ oz Simple Syrup (see here)

¼ oz aquafaba (see Note)

Slice of lemon peel, for garnish

SIMPLE SYRUP Combine sugar and water in a small saucepan and bring just to a boil, stirring frequently, until sugar is fully dissolved. Remove from heat and set aside to cool.

Simple syrup can be stored in a glass jar in the fridge for up to 2 weeks.

OKANAGAN HASKAP SOUR Combine all ingredients in a cocktail shaker. Add 1½ cups of ice and shake, shake, shake for 10 to 12 seconds. Pop open the shaker, discard the ice and shake again without ice for another 10 to 12 seconds. This is known as a "dry shake" and will give you a richer foam.

Double strain (using both a Hawthorne strainer and fine-mesh sieve) into a small rocks glass or a coupe. If you like, add a large ice cube or enjoy the drink "up" with no ice at all. Garnish with a slice of lemon peel.

NOTE Aquafaba is the drained liquid from a can of chickpeas. It is often used as a vegan egg replacer or binder, and it can be whipped into a foam.

HOME BLOCK AT CEDARCREEK ESTATE WINERY

Neil Taylor
KELOWNA

Neil Taylor had never really been to the Okanagan before 2018, when he was approached to open the restaurant at CedarCreek. "I loved everything about the valley," he recalls. "It's only going to become more interesting."

It's not the first time he made a snap decision to move his life and career. Originally from the U.K., he worked at London's famous River Café and was bouncing around the globe—Australia, India, Sri Lanka—when a friend told him someone was opening a restaurant similar to River Café in Vancouver. The restaurant was Cibo Trattoria, which *enRoute* magazine named Canada's best new restaurant of 2008.

"I said I'd do a year and see what happens," he says, then adds, "I never left." After four years at Cibo, he opened the Spanish restaurant España and a pub called the Fat Badger. Along the way, he and his wife also had two kids. "That was a big factor in moving up here," he says. "They love it here. They're really happy."

He is, too. He gets to cook the Mediterranean-inspired cuisine he loves and, with a wood-fired grill and ingredients so fresh, he still marvels

at his luck. "The best stuff—tomatoes and peppers—comes from up here," he says. "We are very blessed with our location to our restaurant."

He also works closely with Taylor Whelan, the talented young winemaker who has taken one of B.C.'s "original eight" estate wineries through an organic transformation. "I let the grapes do the talking," Whelan says. "The food is simple—we buy nice ingredients, and we don't overwork them. The whole thing reminds me of the Mediterranean winery experience."

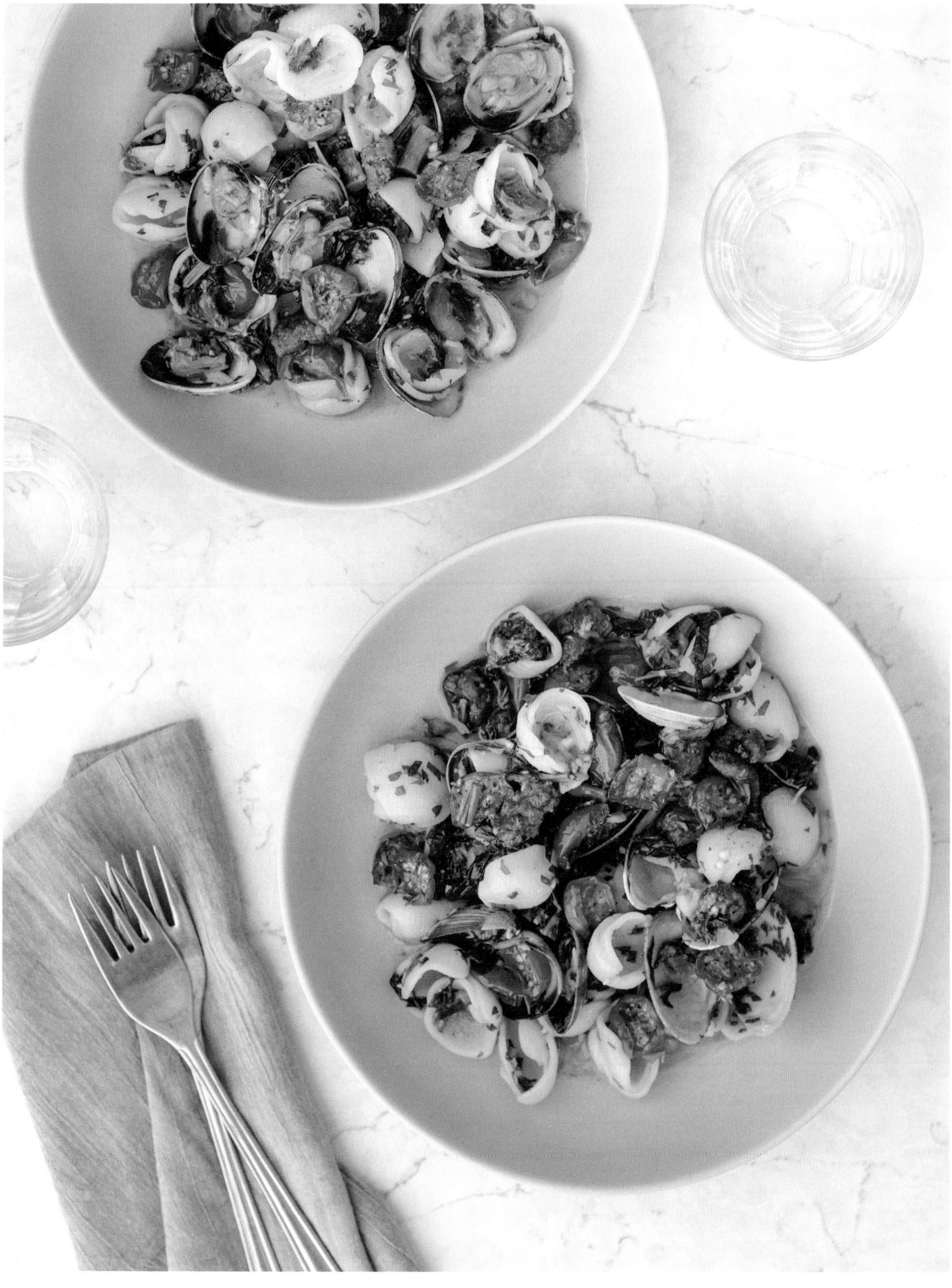

Orecchiette with Manila Clams, Merguez and Rapini, p. 81

Orecchiette with Manila Clams, Merguez and Rapini

The Italian word *orecchiette* means "little ears" and the cup-like shape of this pasta is perfectly designed to embrace the salty-spicy-buttery sauce of this dish by chef Neil Taylor. Merguez is a North African lamb sausage flavoured with earthy and aromatic spices that play beautifully against the brininess of the clams.

Preparation is everything! Be sure to have all ingredients ready as the recipe comes together quickly in the cooking. SERVES 4

CedarCreek Estate
Sauvignon Blanc

Bunch of rapini or broccolini, trimmed and washed well

8 oz dry orecchiette pasta

4 spicy merguez lamb sausages, casings removed, cut into bite-sized pieces

2 Tbsp olive oil

4 salted anchovy fillets, roughly chopped

3 large cloves garlic, finely chopped

1 Tbsp fennel seeds, toasted and ground

32 Manila clams (2 lbs), cleaned and scrubbed (see Note)

½ cup dried cherry tomatoes packed in oil or sun-dried tomatoes in oil, roughly chopped

½ cup CedarCreek Estate Sauvignon Blanc

¼ cup (½ stick) butter, cubed, plus more if needed

Salt and black pepper, to taste

½ lemon

½ bunch Italian parsley, roughly chopped

Peppery olive oil, for finishing

Bring 2 large saucepans of salted water up to a boil.

Add rapini (or broccolini) to one of the pans and cook for 5 minutes, or until stems are just tender to the touch. Drain, then plunge into a cold-water bath to cool. Once cool enough to handle, squeeze out excess water and chop into 1-inch pieces. Set aside.

Add orecchiette into the other saucepan and cook according to package instructions.

Meanwhile, heat a large frying pan over medium heat. Add sausage and sauté for 5 minutes, or until golden and slightly crispy. Reduce heat to medium-low. Add olive oil, anchovies, garlic and fennel seeds. Sauté for another minute or so, until garlic is golden. Add rapini and increase heat to medium.

Stir in clams, tomatoes, wine and butter. Season with salt and pepper and cover with a tight-fitting lid. Cook for 2 to 3 minutes, until clams open up. Discard any unopened clams.

Add a squeeze of lemon juice. Season to taste with more lemon juice. If the sauce looks thin, add a few more knobs of butter and cook for another 1 to 2 minutes.

Drain pasta, reserving ½ cup of pasta water. Add pasta to the pan, sprinkle with parsley and gently toss, until the sauce clings to the pasta. If it looks dry, add a bit of reserved pasta water. If it looks too wet, cook gently over a medium-low heat and let the starch of the pasta thicken the sauce. Season to taste with salt, pepper and more lemon. Serve in warm bowls with a drizzle of peppery olive oil.

NOTE Keep the clams in the fridge, covered with a damp cloth, until needed. Take care to give them one more thorough rinse before using to make sure the shells are grit-free.

Basque-Style Cheesecake with Marmalade Ice Cream, Salted Caramel and Marcona Almonds

Home Block chef Neil Taylor is best known for his Italian cooking, but he loves the foods of Spain just as much—and this indulgent cheesecake is one of the reasons why. As it bakes, the top darkens until it is almost burnt, adding a deeply caramelized flavour to balance all the creamy goodness.

This cheesecake is best served as soon as possible, but it can be refrigerated and served the next day either cold or warmed up briefly in a hot oven. SERVES 6 TO 8

CedarCreek Platinum Riesling Icewine

MARMALADE ICE CREAM

3 to 4 cups premium-quality vanilla ice cream

¼ cup Seville orange marmalade

CHEESECAKE

3 (250-g) packages cream cheese, room temperature

1 cup sugar

1 tsp salt

1 vanilla bean, split lengthwise and seeds scraped

Grated zest of 1 lemon

3 eggs

5 egg yolks

1⅔ cups whipping (33%) cream

Pinch of cinnamon

¼ cup "oo" flour, sifted

¼ cup salted Marcona almonds, lightly crushed, for garnish

SALTED CARAMEL

1 cup soft light brown sugar

¼ cup (½ stick) butter

1¼ cups whipping (33%) cream

1 tsp salt

MARMALADE ICE CREAM Working as quickly as possible, scoop ice cream into a chilled metal mixing bowl and add marmalade. Gently swirl marmalade through ice cream. Return ice cream to container (or pack into a new container) and freeze for at least 1 hour.

CHEESECAKE Preheat oven to 425°F. Line a 9½-inch springform pan with parchment paper and lightly grease it. Set aside.

In a stand mixer fitted with the paddle attachment, combine cream cheese, sugar, salt, vanilla seeds and lemon zest. Mix on medium-high speed for 10 minutes, occasionally stopping to scrape down the sides of the bowl, until mixture is smooth and creamy.

Reduce speed to medium. Slowly add whole eggs, one at a time. Add yolks, one at a time, and mix until eggs are fully incorporated. Reduce speed to low, then add cream and cinnamon. Add flour and mix until combined.

Pour batter into the prepared pan and bake for 25 to 30 minutes, until cheesecake is just set in the middle (but slightly wobbly) and top is a deep golden brown. Remove from oven and let cool to room temperature.

SALTED CARAMEL Meanwhile, heat brown sugar in a heavy-bottomed saucepan over medium heat. Using a heatproof spatula, stir constantly for 5 minutes, or until lightly caramelized. Add butter and cook for a minute until melted. Stir in cream and bring to a boil. (Be careful—it may spatter.) Add salt and increase heat to medium-high. Cook for another 2 to 3 minutes.

Remove pan from heat and set aside to cool to room temperature. (If the sauce solidifies once cooled, gently heat up before using.)

ASSEMBLY Slice cheesecake into 6 to 8 wedges and place on plates. Top with a scoop of marmalade ice cream. Drizzle salted caramel over ice cream and cheesecake, then spoon crushed almonds on top. Serve immediately.

JOJO'S CAFÉ

Joanne Muirhead
OSOYOOS

Main Street in Osoyoos is like something out of time, wide and graceful, designed for big cars with fins and whitewall tires. Buildings are a low-slung mix of Mission, Western and modern styles. Pedestrians meander slowly under the hot sun. The traffic doesn't move much faster.

This is where you'll find Jojo's Café, a place where locals and visitors alike stop in for breakfast sandwiches to go, a quick lunch, a leisurely gossip or an open-mic night for anyone who wants to pick up a sax or guitar. Joanne Muirhead's art-filled space is her second act after a career in wildlife biology. But even while she worked at the Desert Centre up the road, she always thought, "It would be so awesome to open my place, but it was way too scary and way too risky."

Then her beloved father passed away unexpectedly. "I realized life was too short," she says. She already had a business plan worked out, and then "this perfect place came up on Main Street." In 2010, she opened Jojo's.

She'd learned how to bake from both of her grandmothers and her mother and expected to serve only cookies and muffins from her family recipes. "But that's not what happened at all," she says with a laugh. Instead, customers line up for her popular sandwiches, soups and salads as well as baked goods.

"When I'm baking all these years later, I feel like I'm giving something from my heart," she says. "When you open a place, you think about the big questions in life. I'm just slinging coffee, but I'm also making people happy."

House Granola

"This recipe is super versatile," says Jojo's owner Joanne Muirhead. "You can use any kind of nut and dried fruit." She points out that it's gluten-free and vegan, too, as long as honey is accepted in your vegan diet. Enjoy it with milk, yogurt and/or fresh fruit—or, for a more decadent treat, crumbled over ice cream. MAKES 8 CUPS

 Matcha Latte or Cappuccino

½ cup vegetable or canola oil
¾ cup brown sugar
¾ cup honey
3 tsp vanilla extract
1 tsp ground cinnamon
½ tsp salt
4½ cups oats
1½ cups whole nuts (almonds, walnuts, hazelnuts and/or cashews)
1½ cups sliced almonds
1½ cups unsweetened shredded coconut
½ cup sunflower seeds
¾ cup dried cranberries
¾ cup raisins

Preheat oven to 300°F. Line 2 baking sheets with parchment paper.

Combine oil, brown sugar, honey, vanilla, cinnamon and salt in a large bowl. Mix well.

Stir in oats, nuts, coconut and seeds. (Do not add the fruit.) Spread mixture in a single layer onto the prepared baking sheets. Bake for 15 minutes, then stir well. Bake for another 15 minutes, until granola is golden brown. Stir again. Set aside to cool on the pan. The granola will crisp up once it cools.

Add dried fruit and mix well.

Store granola for up to 6 months in the freezer or keep it in a zip-top bag in the fridge to keep it crunchy.

Oatmeal Raisin or Chocolate Chip Cookies

Joanne Muirhead's dad was "a connoisseur of cookies," and these were his favourite. "When we bake cookies at the café, real love goes into them and that makes all the difference in the world," Muirhead says. MAKES ABOUT 12 LARGE COOKIES

 Vin Santo or Port

1 cup (2 sticks) butter, room temperature

1 cup packed brown sugar

¾ cup sugar

2 eggs

1 tsp vanilla extract

2 cups oats

2 cups Rice Krispies

2 cups unsweetened shredded coconut, toasted

1 cup flour

1 tsp baking powder

½ tsp baking soda

1 tsp salt

3 cups raisins or chocolate chips (or 1½ cups of each to make a half batch of each flavour)

Preheat oven to 350°F. Line 2 baking sheets with parchment paper.

In a stand mixer fitted with a paddle attachment, beat butter until it's light and creamy. (Alternatively, use a bowl and hand mixer.) Add both sugars and beat until smooth and creamy. Mix in eggs and vanilla and beat again.

Add oats, Rice Krispies, coconut, flour, baking powder, baking soda and salt and mix on low speed. Add raisins (or chocolate chips) to the dough. If you are making both kinds of cookies, divide dough in half and stir raisins into one half and chocolate chips into the other half.

Using a ¼-cup scoop, scoop dough into tight, even-sized balls. Place on the prepared baking sheets, about 2 inches apart, and press down to form a cookie shape. Bake for 10 minutes, or until edges are slightly browned and centres are nearly baked. Set aside to cool on the sheet for 10 minutes, then transfer cookies to a cooling rack.

KARAT

Julian Helman

KELOWNA

Julian Helman's friends weren't so confident back in 2016 when the pastry chef started making his painstakingly painted, moulded and filled creations in the basement of Mission Hill Family Estate Winery (page 166).

"Even close friends and chefs were sceptical about trying to create something higher end in Kelowna, but we've left our thumbprint and we are still doing what we love," he says happily. Originally from Saskatoon, Helman had worked in Michelin-starred fine-dining restaurants in Europe and Asia and competed nationally and internationally. Then a friend invited him to the Okanagan. He thought he'd stay a summer. That was a decade ago.

He was working at Quails' Gate in 2016 when he decided to make and sell handcrafted chocolates at Christmas, many to friends and co-workers, who provided part of the seed money to start his company. "I had $400 in my bank account at the time. I took that $400 and invested in a couple bags of chocolate and I spent $30 to register the business," he recalls. His first customer was Mission Hill owner Anthony von Mandl, looking for a gift for his mother's ninetieth birthday. "I made $1,200 that first season and I just kept going."

And so Karat was born. Helman opened a tiny commercial kitchen, followed by a bakery café in 2018, and has built a team of eighteen "warriors." In addition to his hand-painted chocolates, he sells chocolate bars like the wine-infused Terroir Bar as well as pastries in the European-style café.

"After doing pastry so long, chocolate became my nearest and dearest obsession, where I wanted to learn all about it," he says.

Tempura Chocolate Fondants

Julian Helman has been making this chocolate fondant recipe for years and says, "It's been experimented with and remodelled many times over. It's tried and true and my favourite version is this dark chocolate recipe." His latest variation is a fried tempura-style. "I don't know what possessed me to try this—it sounded like it would taste yummy," he says. SERVES 8

 Tantalus Pinot Noir

CHOCOLATE FONDANTS

21 oz bittersweet dark chocolate (preferably Valrhona Guanaja 70%), chopped

⅔ cup (1½ sticks) butter, plus extra for greasing

¾ cup sugar

⅓ cup heavy (36%) cream

9 eggs, room temperature

9 egg yolks, room temperature

¾ cup flour

Unsweetened cocoa powder, for dusting, if needed

TEMPURA BATTER

1 cup flour

1 cup cornstarch

1 tsp baking powder

2 eggs

2 Tbsp canola oil

1½ cups club soda

TEMPURA CHOCOLATE FONDANTS

8 cups canola oil

Chocolate Fondants, still frozen (see here)

2 eggs

¼ cup milk

1 cup flour, or as needed

Tempura Batter (see here)

ASSEMBLY

Ice cream, whipped cream, fruit purée and/or berries, to serve

CHOCOLATE FONDANTS Place chocolate in a stainless steel bowl over a saucepan of simmering water and melt slowly, stirring constantly to avoid scorching chocolate. (Alternatively, microwave 30 seconds at a time, stirring in between.)

In a small saucepan, combine butter, sugar and cream. Bring to a simmer over medium heat, taking care not to let it boil or burn. Pour hot cream over chocolate and stir vigorously to create a ganache. Allow mixture to cool to room temperature. Using a whisk, mix in eggs and yolks, one at a time. Work quickly but try not to incorporate too much air. Sift flour into the mixture and mix again.

Scoop or pipe the mixture into 8 cavities in a non-stick silicone muffin or cupcake mould, dividing the batter equally. Freeze for about 4 hours.

NOTE If you are serving the fondants without the tempura coating, preheat oven to 400°F and do not scoop the fondant into the silicone baking mould. Instead, generously grease eight 3- x 1-inch ramekins and dust with cocoa powder. Arrange on a baking sheet to make it easier to transfer in and out of the oven.

Scoop fondant into the prepared ramekins. Bake for 10 to 12 minutes. Set aside to cool until just warm to the touch.

TEMPURA BATTER Whisk all ingredients together in a large bowl. Place in the fridge to chill until needed.

TEMPURA CHOCOLATE FONDANTS Pour oil into a deep fryer or deep saucepan and heat to a temperature of 350°F. (The oil should be at least 3 inches deep with lots of room at the top as it will bubble furiously once the battered fondants are added.)

Keep fondants frozen in the freezer until needed. In a small bowl, whisk eggs and milk. Place flour in a separate bowl. Bring the bowl of batter from the fridge to the counter. Line up the three bowls in order, near the stovetop.

Remove a frozen chocolate fondant from the freezer. Working quickly, dip the frozen fondant in the egg wash, ensuring it is well coated. Dust it in flour, then dip in the batter. Carefully lower the fondant into the pan, taking care not to splash hot oil. Repeat with a couple more, frying a few at a time. Deep-fry for 6 minutes until crispy. Using a slotted spoon, transfer the fondants to a paper towel–lined plate to drain. Repeat with remaining fondants.

ASSEMBLY Serve tempura fondants immediately. If serving plain fondants, place a plate, top-side down, over each ramekin, then invert to release the cakes. Serve either version with your choice of ice cream, whipped cream, fruit purée and/or berries.

Milk Chocolate Mousse with Salted Caramel

Who doesn't love chocolate mousse? Chef Julian Helman takes the classic dessert—simply a chocolate ganache mixed with whipped cream—and makes it extraordinary with salted caramel, crunchy sponge toffee and a hint of Okanagan Spirits BRBN. This appealing bourbon-style whisky is made from B.C. corn and won gold at the 2022 Canadian Whisky Awards. SERVES 8

 Okanagan Spirits BRBN

CHOCOLATE MOUSSE
- 11 oz milk chocolate (preferably Valrhona Jivara 40%), chopped
- 2 sheets silver gelatin or vegan plant-based gelatin
- 1 cup milk, almond milk or oat milk
- 1 vanilla bean, split lengthwise and seeds scraped
- 2 Tbsp Okanagan Spirits BRBN whisky
- 2 cups whipping (33%) cream or coconut cream

SPONGE TOFFEE
- 1¼ cups sugar
- 3 Tbsp water
- 2 Tbsp light corn syrup
- ½ Tbsp vanilla extract
- 1½ Tbsp baking soda

SALTED CARAMEL
- ½ cup heavy (36%) cream
- 2 Tbsp glucose syrup (see Note)
- 2 Tbsp Okanagan Spirits BRBN whisky
- ½ tsp salt
- 1 Tbsp vanilla extract
- ⅔ cup sugar
- 2 Tbsp butter, room temperature

ASSEMBLY
- Whipped cream (optional)
- Chocolate shavings or cacao nibs (optional)

CHOCOLATE MOUSSE Place chocolate in a large bowl. Bloom gelatin in cold water.

Place milk (or milk alternative) and vanilla seeds and bean in a small saucepan. Bring to a simmer over medium heat. Discard bean, then add gelatin to the mixture and stir until dissolved.

Pour hot milk over chocolate, then add whisky and whisk until smooth. Cool ganache to 30°C.

Whip cream to soft peaks. Fold cream into chocolate in three additions.

Pour into serving glasses or bowls and chill in the fridge.

SPONGE TOFFEE Line a 12-inch square baking pan, at least 2 inches deep, with parchment paper.

Fit a deep, medium saucepan with a candy thermometer. Add sugar, water and corn syrup and cook over medium heat to 150°C (hard-crack stage), stirring often but taking care not to let the sugar splash the sides.

Working quickly and carefully—hot sugar can be dangerous—remove from heat. Whisk in vanilla and baking soda. It will foam up dramatically.

Pour into the prepared baking pan. Allow to cool to room temperature.

SALTED CARAMEL In a small saucepan, combine cream, glucose syrup, whisky, salt and vanilla. Cook over medium heat just until the mixture comes to a simmer, about 10 minutes, then reduce heat to medium-low and keep warm.

Heat a large saucepan over medium-low heat. Add 1 tablespoon sugar at a time and stir with a wooden spoon until melted. Cook for 10 minutes, or until golden brown and caramelized.

Working quickly and carefully, stir the warm cream mixture into the caramelized sugar. Attach a candy thermometer to the side of the saucepan and simmer until the mixture reaches a temperature of 102.8°C. Remove from heat and let cool to 37.8°C. Whisk in butter.

NOTE Glucose syrup is used in commercial baking to sweeten and thicken baked goods and keep them moist. If you can't find it, in most cases you can use corn syrup instead.

ASSEMBLY Remove chocolate mousse from the fridge. Pour cooled caramel sauce on top. If using, top with whipped cream and chocolate shavings (or cacao nibs).

Break up small pieces of sponge toffee and arrange on top. (It's important to do this just before serving so they stay crisp.)

KLIPPERS ORGANICS

Kevin and Annamarie Klippenstein
CAWSTON

Kevin Klippenstein still remembers going for dinner at his then-girlfriend Annamarie's family farm in the Fraser Valley two decades ago. "I'd go to a barbecue at her parents' house and ask myself why the steak tasted so good or the peach tasted so different," he says.

What made that steak and that peach so delicious was that they were farmed organically, a rarity in B.C. at the time. So when the newlywed Klippensteins started their own five-acre farm in the Similkameen Valley, there was never any question that it, too, would be organic.

"I don't know any different," says Annamarie. "Why would I grow something that I wouldn't consume myself? Why would I feed something to my trees and plants that I wouldn't drink myself? I've always been super passionate about this."

Turns out, plenty of other people were, too. "We thought five acres was a good amount of land, and we quickly found that it wasn't enough," Kevin says. Now with sixty acres, half of it ground crops and half fruit trees, Klippers has become one of the most sought-after names at Vancouver's farmers' markets and fine-dining restaurants.

But Klippers also has guest suites, education, Untangled Craft Cider, the celebrated Row Fourteen restaurant (page 140) and, since 2021, a café and market best known for Buddha bowls, breakfast sandwiches, baked goods and fresh veggies to load into the cooler for the drive home.

"The store has been great," says Annamarie. "A lot of people just want a quick bite to eat, something healthy and nutritious. Everything is made from scratch from ingredients we know and trust." And, she adds, "If everyone can leave with a tidbit of information that connects us with food, [I've achieved] my goal."

Buddha Bowl, p. 94

Buddha Bowl

People look to Klippers Organics for healthy food they can enjoy on the go, and this Buddha bowl is a perennial favourite. Its ingredients change with the seasons, but this vegan and gluten-free version is sure to satisfy. Most of the ingredients can be prepared ahead of time and assembled when you're hungry. Falafel made with dried chickpeas taste better than canned but require slightly more effort—start it the night before you plan to serve it. SERVES 4

Untangled Craft Cider
Tangled Apple Cider

FALAFEL

2 cups dried chickpeas
    or 2 (15-oz) cans
2 cloves garlic
½ small onion, sliced (¼ cup)
2 Tbsp raw sesame seeds
1 to 2 beets, grated (½ cup)
1 Tbsp ground cumin
1½ tsp salt
¼ tsp cayenne pepper
Black pepper, to taste
1 Tbsp lemon juice
¼ cup chickpea flour

SWEET AND SPICY
KABOCHA SQUASH

1 kabocha squash, peeled,
    halved, seeded and
    cut into ½-inch cubes
1 Tbsp olive oil
¼ cup brown sugar
1 tsp ground cumin
½ tsp cayenne pepper
½ tsp ground cinnamon
¼ tsp ground nutmeg
½ tsp salt

FALAFEL If using dried chickpeas, soak in a bowl of water overnight.

Preheat oven to 400°F. Line a baking sheet with parchment paper.

Drain chickpeas and rinse well. Place in a food processor, then add garlic, onions and sesame seeds. Pulse until mixture is finely chopped but not mush. Add beets, spices and lemon juice and process again until well incorporated. Add chickpea flour and pulse until well combined.

Give the mixture a good stir with a spatula. Shape into 8 balls (about 2 tablespoons each) and flatten slightly. Transfer to the prepared baking sheet and bake for 17 minutes. Flip, then bake for another 15 to 18 minutes. Set aside to cool to room temperature.

Falafels can be stored in the fridge for up to 5 days or uncooked in the freezer for up to 3 months. To prepare from frozen, thaw out and bake as above.

SWEET AND SPICY KABOCHA SQUASH
Preheat oven to 400°F. Line a baking sheet with parchment paper.

Place squash and oil in a large bowl and toss.

In a small bowl, combine remaining ingredients. Sprinkle half of the spice blend over the squash and gently mix.

Spread out squash on the baking sheet in a single layer. Sprinkle half of the remaining spice blend over the squash and bake for 15 minutes. Turn squash over and sprinkle the remaining spice blend on top. Bake for another 10 minutes. Remove from the oven and set aside to cool.

TOMATO-TOASTED PUMPKIN SEEDS

½ cup shelled pumpkin seeds

1 tsp olive oil

1 Tbsp sun-dried tomato powder (see Note)

¼ tsp sea salt

SUN-DRIED TOMATO TAHINI DRESSING

1 large clove garlic

½ cup raw sesame seeds

¼ cup sun-dried tomato powder

¼ tsp salt

¼ tsp black pepper

¾ cup olive oil

½ cup cold water

½ cup apple cider vinegar

2 Tbsp lemon juice

1 Tbsp maple syrup

ASSEMBLY

2 cups cooked tricolour quinoa

1 large carrot, grated

1 large beet, grated

1 watermelon radish, thinly sliced

1 cucumber, sliced

TOMATO-TOASTED PUMPKIN SEEDS
Preheat oven to 350°F. Line a baking sheet with parchment paper.

In a small bowl, combine pumpkin seeds and oil and toss. Stir in tomato powder and salt.

Transfer to the prepared baking sheet and roast for 4 minutes. Mix and roast for another 3 minutes. Set aside to cool.

NOTE You can purchase sun-dried tomato powder online or at specialty grocers. You can also substitute it with regular tomato powder or make your own by dehydrating tomatoes in the sun, the oven or a dehydrator until they are hard and brittle. Using a blender or food processor, grind into a powder.

SUN-DRIED TOMATO TAHINI DRESSING
Place all ingredients in a blender and blend until smooth.

ASSEMBLY Divide quinoa between 4 bowls. Pile on carrots, beets, and slices of radish and cucumber. Break up falafels and add to the bowls. Top with squash. Drizzle with the dressing and garnish with toasted pumpkin seeds.

Creamy Vegan
Heirloom Tomato Soup

The Similkameen Valley's hot dry days, windy afternoons and cool nights are ideal for nightshades such as eggplants, peppers and especially tomatoes. The tomatoes from Klippers Organics are renowned among chefs and this vegan recipe makes the most of them. Best of all, you can freeze the tomatoes when they are in season, then make this soup any time of year—or you can freeze the soup itself and have it ready for a taste of summer on a wintry day. SERVES 8

Untangled Craft Cider
Black Plum Basil Cider

HEIRLOOM TOMATO SOUP

5 lbs fresh or frozen heirloom tomatoes (thawed if frozen), quartered

¼ cup loosely packed basil leaves

¼ cup olive oil

1 onion, chopped

2 carrots, chopped

1 cup water

2 Tbsp organic cane sugar or honey, plus extra to taste

1 tsp sea salt, plus extra to taste

½ tsp black pepper, plus extra to taste

Pinch of cayenne pepper, plus extra to taste

⅓ cup raw cashews

VEGAN PESTO

8 cups basil leaves

2 cups shelled pumpkin seeds

1¼ cups nutritional yeast

½ tsp salt

1¼ cups olive oil

⅓ cup lemon juice

ASSEMBLY

Vegan Pesto (see here)

Tomato-Toasted Pumpkin Seeds (see page 94)

Cherry tomatoes, halved

HEIRLOOM TOMATO SOUP Place tomatoes in a saucepan and bring to a boil. Cook over medium heat for 30 minutes. Add basil and cook for another 5 minutes. Working in batches if needed, transfer to a high-speed blender and purée until smooth. Strain through a fine-mesh sieve to remove skins and pulp, then set puréed tomatoes aside.

Heat oil in a heavy-bottomed pan over medium-high heat. Add onions and sauté for 3 to 4 minutes until softened. Add carrots, then reduce heat to medium and sauté for 3 to 4 minutes, until onions are golden.

Add puréed tomatoes, water, sugar (or honey), salt, black pepper, cayenne and cashews. Stir, increase heat and bring to a simmer. Cover, then reduce heat to low and gently simmer for 10 to 15 minutes, until carrots are tender. Remove from heat.

Using an immersion blender, blend until smooth. Season to taste with a little more salt, black pepper, sugar and cayenne. Soup can be stored in the fridge for 5 days or in the freezer for 6 months.

VEGAN PESTO Place all ingredients in a blender or food processor and blend until creamy. Pesto can be stored in the fridge for 5 days.

ASSEMBLY To serve, ladle soup into bowls and top with vegan pesto, pumpkin seeds and cherry tomatoes.

LEGEND DISTILLING

Dawn and Doug Lennie
NARAMATA

It was only a matter of time before someone realized that all that flavourful Naramata fruit would
taste even better in local spirits.

"We use a lot of Naramata fruit and botani-
cals," says Dawn Lennie, who co-owns Legend
Distilling with her husband Doug. That could mean
the apples in their signature Doctor's Orders Gin,
sumac berries in the Manitou Orange & Sumac
Liqueur and Naramata honey in the Honey Moon
Gin. "Then we have a Cosmo Martini in a bottle
where we use cranberries from the Lower Main-
land and Naramata-grown raspberries," she adds.

The Lennies started Legend Distilling in 2014,
shortly after the province relaxed its rules (and,
importantly, its onerous tax structure) around craft
distilling. Before that, they'd owned The Bench
Market in Penticton, which Dawn and her sister
founded in 2005.

"We wanted to do something in Naramata.
We looked at what was here and were interested
in distilling," Dawn says. They hatched their plan in
2009 and Doug trained at a couple distilleries in
the U.S. Once they found their perfect location
(Naramata's former doctor's office), they invested
in a 600-litre copper still and two columns.

They've since produced more than a dozen
gins, vodkas, liqueurs and ready-to-pour cocktails,
most attached with a quirky story. The Shadow in
the Lake Vodka, for instance, refers to the legend
of Ogopogo.

And now, finally, there's Wyatt Whisky.

"Whisky is a big thing for Doug, one of his
passions," Dawn says. They are especially excited
about an upcoming six-year release, distilled from
Peace River wheat and rye, and aged in former
wine and cherry Port barrels from neighbouring
wineries. "It speaks to the terroir of our area."

Blueberry-Basil Punch, p. 101 and Lavender Lemonade Cocktail, p. 100

Lavender Lemonade Cocktail

At Legend Distilling, Doctor's Orders Gin is good for what ails you. This contemporary-style gin flavoured with local apple, elderberry and lavender notes is designed to work in a G&T, martini or Negroni, but it might be at its best in this refreshing summery cocktail. The base ingredients—the lavender tea, lemonade and simple syrup—can all be made ahead of time and kept on hand to serve whenever the thirst takes you. SERVES 1

LAVENDER TEA

4 cups water

½ cup culinary lavender, cleaned and sifted

LAVENDER LEMONADE BASE

4 cups Lavender Tea (see here)

½ cup simple syrup (see Note)

½ cup lemon juice

LAVENDER LEMONADE

1 oz Doctor's Orders Gin

3 to 4 oz Lavender Lemonade Base (see here)

Lemon peel, for garnish

Sprig of lavender, for garnish

LAVENDER TEA Bring the water to a boil in a saucepan. Stir in lavender. Remove from heat and let steep for 30 minutes. Strain, then allow to cool to room temperature.

Transfer to a glass jar or pitcher and chill until needed. Tea can be stored in the fridge for up to 2 weeks.

LAVENDER LEMONADE BASE Combine all ingredients in a glass jar or pitcher and mix well. Refrigerate for up to 5 days.

LAVENDER LEMONADE Fill a rocks or Collins glass with ice. Add gin and top with lavender lemonade base. Garnish with lemon peel and lavender.

If you're serving a crowd, fill a pitcher with ice, add 8 ounces gin and top with lavender lemonade mix. Serve in punch cups or rocks glasses.

NOTE To make simple syrup, bring 1 cup each sugar and water just to a boil and stir until sugar is fully dissolved. Remove from heat and cool. Sugar syrup can be stored in the fridge for 2 weeks.

Blueberry-Basil Punch

This fruity, slightly herbal punch really packs a, well, you know. That's thanks to Legend Distilling's flagship Shadow in the Lake Vodka. This wheat-based spirit is smooth and full-bodied with notes of vanilla and caramel. The name refers to the Ogopogo, a sacred spirit the Syilx and Secwépemc people call Naitaka, who is believed to live in Okanagan Lake. SERVES 8

BLUEBERRY-BASIL SYRUP AND FRUIT LEATHER

1½ heaping cups blueberries

15 large basil leaves, torn

1 cup water

1 cup sugar

BLUEBERRY-BASIL PUNCH

4 cups water

2 cups Blueberry-Basil Syrup (see here)

1 cup Shadow in the Lake vodka

¼ cup lemon juice

¼ cup lime juice

Sprigs of basil, for garnish

Blueberry-Basil Fruit Leather (see here), for garnish

BLUEBERRY-BASIL SYRUP AND FRUIT LEATHER Preheat oven to 200°F. Line a baking sheet with parchment paper.

Combine all ingredients in a large saucepan and bring to a boil over medium heat. Stirring occasionally, cook for 5 minutes, until blueberries have darkened and start to break down.

Strain syrup into a bowl and reserve for later. (The syrup can be prepared ahead of time and frozen for up to 3 months.)

Transfer the blueberries and basil into a blender or food processor and blend to a jam-like consistency. Spread mixture thinly over the prepared baking sheet and dehydrate in the oven for 3 to 4 hours, until dark and leathery. Set aside to cool to room temperature. Cut into bite-sized pieces.

BLUEBERRY-BASIL PUNCH Combine all ingredients except the garnishes in a large pitcher, drink dispenser or punch bowl. Stir, then chill in the fridge until ready to serve.

Just before serving, add as much ice as possible to keep it cold without risk of too much dilution. Serve over additional ice in rocks glasses or punch cups. Garnish with basil and fruit leather.

THE MODEST BUTCHER

Dan Carkner
WEST KELOWNA

Mt. Boucherie Winery has sweeping views of Okanagan Lake in its front yard and an extinct volcano in the back. In between is The Modest Butcher, where chef Dan Carkner exchanges dad-jokey quips as handily as he flips steaks and burgers.

"We're a winery restaurant, but that doesn't mean you can't come in for a beer sometimes," he says, adding, "It means we chefs have to taste the wine. It's really tough, but we struggle through."

Originally from Ottawa, Carkner fell into cooking by accident, washing dishes at a Banff steak house to finance his ski-bum lifestyle. He spent a couple years cooking at Mission Hill (page 166), attended culinary school in P.E.I. and returned home to work in the white-glove Parliamentary Dining Room. But Kelowna was calling him back, and he returned to wine country in 2018. "It took some time, but I'm thankful it all fell into place," he says.

The Mt. Boucherie property was planted with vines as far back as 1968, although it didn't start releasing its own wines until 2001. In 2016, it was purchased by Vancouver businessman Sonny Huang, who launched a massive makeover. The Modest Butcher was a major part of that rebrand, and with a name like "Boucherie"—French for "butcher shop"—it's no surprise that steak is on the menu.

They're as much neighbourhood hangout as destination restaurant, justly famous for their burger. "If you want to go all out, you can have a tomahawk steak and a high-end wine and really swing for the fences," he notes. "Before living in Kelowna, I'd never experienced any place like this, where food and wine go together hand in hand."

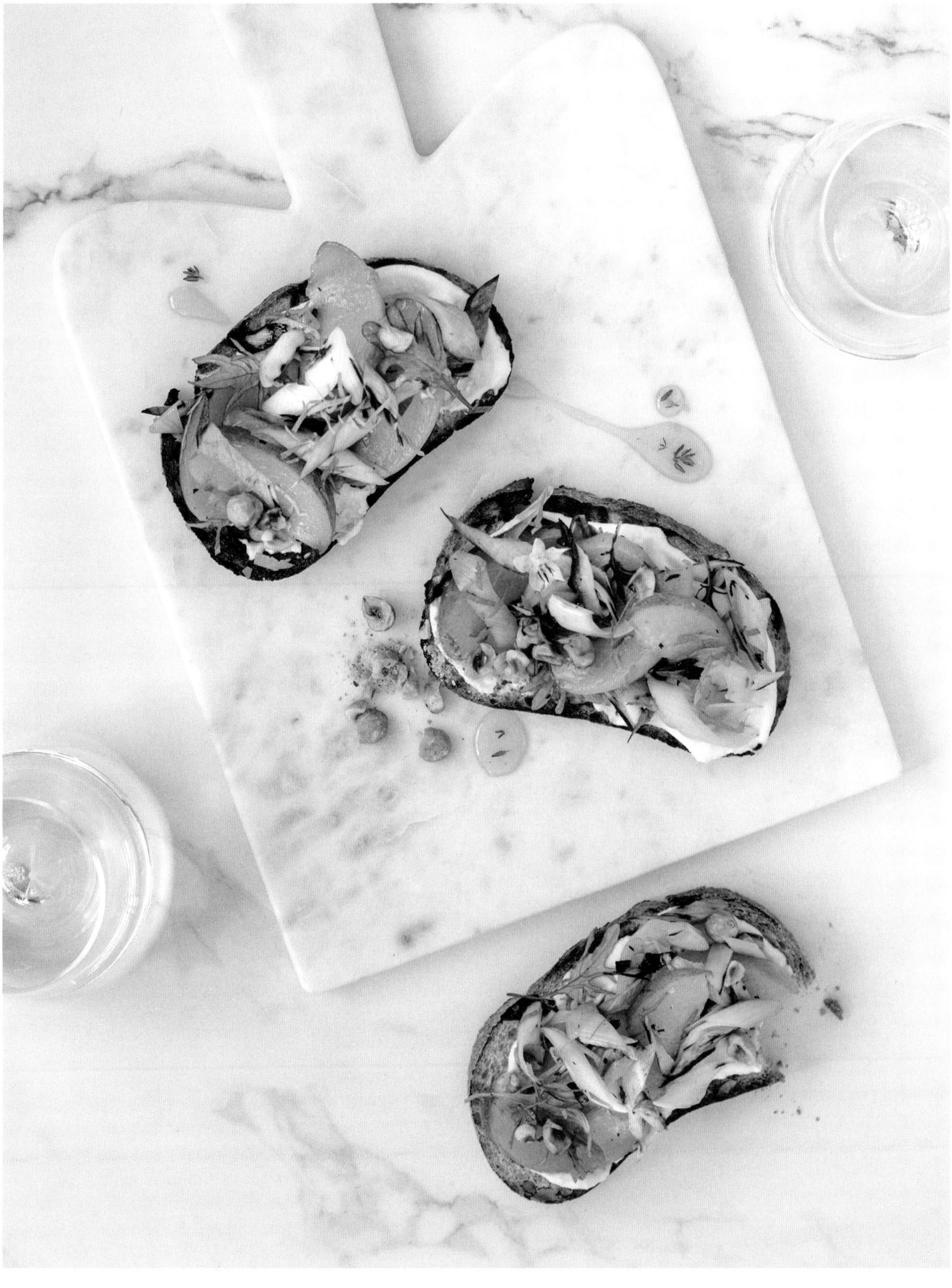

Things on Toast, p. 104

Things on Toast

At The Modest Butcher, one of the most popular dishes is Things on Toast, an open-faced sandwich that changes as the seasons do, topped with whatever is fresh and delicious right now. This incarnation is prepared with quick-pickled Okanagan peaches, grilled leeks, toasted hazelnuts, whipped goat feta and a thyme-scented white wine gastrique. SERVES 4

Mt. Boucherie Original Vines Chardonnay

QUICK-PICKLED OKANAGAN PEACHES

3 to 4 cloves garlic, crushed

4 cups white vinegar

2 cups water

2 cups sugar

1 Tbsp salt

1 Tbsp pickling spice

¼ cup chopped dill

4 to 6 near-ripe Okanagan peaches, cut into ½-inch-thick wedges

THYME-SCENTED GASTRIQUE

1 small onion, roughly chopped

4 cloves garlic, lightly smashed

¼ cup sliced, peeled ginger

Pinch of salt

2 star anise

1 cinnamon stick

10 to 12 sprigs thyme

1 cup Mt. Boucherie Pinot Gris

2 cups sugar

1 cup apple cider vinegar

Grated zest and juice of 1 orange

QUICK-PICKLED OKANAGAN PEACHES Combine garlic, vinegar, water, sugar, salt and pickling spice in a large saucepan. Bring to a simmer and stir until sugar and salt have dissolved. Remove the pan from the heat. Stir in dill.

Place peaches in a non-reactive bowl, and set inside a larger bowl or sink filled with ice.

Pour enough pickling liquid over the peaches to cover. (The ice under the bowl will cool things quickly so the peaches don't get mushy.) Set aside to cool to room temperature. Store the pickled peaches in an airtight container or Mason jars, ensuring they are completely submerged in the pickling liquid, for up to 3 weeks.

NOTE Carkner adds that the quick pickling method here works well for most garden veggies: radishes, cucumbers, onions, carrots or a combination.

THYME-SCENTED GASTRIQUE Combine onions, garlic, ginger and salt in a heavy-bottomed saucepan. Heat over medium-high heat for 5 minutes, stirring occasionally, or until well caramelized. Add star anise, cinnamon and thyme. Sauté for 1 to 2 minutes until aromatic. Pour in wine, scraping up any browned bits from the bottom of the saucepan.

Add sugar, vinegar and the orange juice and zest and simmer for 15 to 20 minutes until sauce is thick and syrupy. If it isn't thick enough, cook a little longer; if it is too thick, thin out with a little water. (You are aiming for a maple syrup consistency.)

Strain through a fine-mesh sieve, pressing out the goodness to make sure you get it all.

WHIPPED GOAT FETA

2 cups Okanagan goat feta
(preferably Carmelis)

Pinch of black pepper, plus
extra to taste

½ cup heavy (36%) cream

Grated lemon zest or
chopped herbs (optional)

Salt, to taste

ASSEMBLY

1 cup hazelnuts

2 leeks, white and light
green parts only,
halved lengthwise
and rinsed well

Olive oil, for drizzling

Salt and black pepper,
to taste

4 slices rustic sourdough

¼ cup Whipped Goat Feta
(see here)

16 slices Quick-Pickled
Okanagan Peaches
(see here)

¼ cup Thyme-Scented
Gastrique (see here)

Microgreens, edible flowers
or baby lettuces,
for garnish (optional)

WHIPPED GOAT FETA Place feta into a food processor and pulse until crumbled. Add pepper. With the motor still running, quickly add in heavy cream. Blend until spreadable, occasionally scraping down the sides. Add lemon zest or herbs (if using). Season to taste with salt and pepper.

Whipped feta can be stored in an airtight container in the fridge for up to a week.

ASSEMBLY Preheat a grill over high heat.

Toast hazelnuts in a dry frying pan for 8 to 10 minutes, until light brown and fragrant. Remove the skins and coarsely crumble under a heavy pan.

Pat leeks dry, then season with oil, salt and pepper. Grill leeks for 1 to 2 minutes per side, until lightly coloured. Transfer to a chopping board and set aside until cool enough to handle. Chop and keep warm.

Drizzle oil over each slice of bread and season with salt and pepper. Carefully toast on the grill, taking care not to burn. Remove bread from the grill and spread with whipped goat feta. Place on individual plates or a serving platter and top with grilled leeks, pickled peaches and toasted hazelnuts. Drizzle with gastrique. Garnish with microgreens, edible flowers or baby lettuces (if using).

Gluten-Free Brownie Trifle

Traditionally a trifle is assembled in one big dish and scooped at the table, but these components look great in jars or on individual plates. As chef Dan Carkner says, "Get a little artsy with the presentation—anything goes!" SERVES 6

Mt. Boucherie
Merlot Icewine

GLUTEN-FREE ESPRESSO BROWNIES

¾ cup (1½ sticks) butter, plus extra for greasing
1 cup rice flour
2 Tbsp unsweetened cocoa powder
1 tsp baking soda
½ tsp salt
1¼ cups (220 g) semi-sweet chocolate (preferably Callebaut)
4 free-range eggs
2 tsp vanilla extract
1 cup sugar
¼ cup hot espresso

DARK CHOCOLATE SAUCE

1½ cups sugar
½ cup unsweetened cocoa powder
¼ tsp salt
1 cup water
1½ tsp vanilla extract

SUMMIT BERRY COMPOTE

2½ cups Mt. Boucherie Summit wine
1 cup sugar
14 oz frozen mixed berries (about 2 cups)
½ cinnamon stick
1 star anise

VANILLA WHIP

2¼ cups heavy (36%) cream
2 Tbsp sugar
1 tsp vanilla extract

ASSEMBLY

Mint leaves, torn, for garnish
Candied pecans, meringue and/or toasted marshmallows, for garnish (optional)

GLUTEN-FREE ESPRESSO BROWNIES Preheat oven to 350°F. Lightly grease a 9- x 13-inch baking pan and line with parchment paper.

In a medium bowl, whisk together rice flour, cocoa powder, baking soda and salt. Set aside.

Over a double boiler, gently melt chocolate and butter over low heat until smooth and glossy. Remove from heat and set aside to cool to near room temperature. Whisk in eggs and vanilla. Stir in sugar and espresso and mix thoroughly.

Fold in dry ingredients in three additions until just mixed.

Pour batter into the prepared pan and smooth the surface. Bake for 20 to 24 minutes, until edges are set and centre is slightly underdone. Set aside to cool. (The residual heat should set the centre as it cools.) Cut into ½-inch cubes.

DARK CHOCOLATE SAUCE In a saucepan, whisk together sugar, cocoa powder and salt. Add water and bring to a boil. Reduce heat to medium-low and simmer for 30 seconds. Remove from heat, then stir in vanilla. Set aside to cool completely.

SUMMIT BERRY COMPOTE In a small saucepan, combine wine and sugar and simmer over medium heat until sugar has dissolved. Add frozen berries, cinnamon stick and star anise. Simmer gently for another 20 to 30 minutes, until thick and syrupy. Remove cinnamon stick and star anise and set aside to cool completely.

VANILLA WHIP Pour cream into a chilled stainless bowl and whisk until soft peaks form. While whisking continuously, gradually add sugar and stir in vanilla. To ensure soft peaks remain, whip a bit more.

ASSEMBLY Add a 1-inch layer of brownie squares to 6 (250-mL) Mason jars. Top with a drizzle of chocolate sauce, then a spoonful of compote and a dollop of vanilla whip. Repeat.

Garnish with mint leaves. Top with candied pecans, meringue and/or toasted marshmallows (if using).

NARAMATA INN

Ned Bell, Stacy Johnston and Minette Lotz
NARAMATA

Ned Bell likes to talk about "taste of place."

"I wanted to be able to say that you could only have this dinner at the Naramata Inn. You couldn't have it anywhere else," he says. "We're not doing anything unique. We're doing something uniquely here."

Bell is executive chef of this "restaurant with rooms," and co-owner with his wife Kate Colley and their business partners Paul Hollands and Maria Wiesner. They first talked about taking over the heritage building back in 2017, and in February 2020 the inn was theirs.

In some ways it was perfect timing. The Four Seasons Vancouver, where Bell had been executive chef for nine years, had just closed, and his contract at Ocean Wise had just ended. (He's now their chef ambassador.) But then came COVID-19, and they were closed before they could even open.

The pandemic gave them time to renovate, adding warm, contemporary decor to the circa 1907 Mission-style hotel, and entice a "dream team" including wine director Emily Walker (page 12), chef de cuisine Stacy Johnston and her wife, forager Minette Lotz, to this charming village at the end of the road.

Together, they have created a culinary program committed to using only ingredients grown in B.C.—and the closer to the inn, the better. Even the Dirty Martini is made with pickled scapes instead of olives.

"We call it French Naramatian—French in style but with local ingredients," says Johnston, who has loved "learning not even the seasonality but the micro-seasonality" of this bountiful region.

For Bell, who was born just up the winding road in Penticton, this has been the happiest of homecomings. And he's not done. "It's not five-star Relais & Château—yet," he says.

Orchard Salad with Poached Pears, Endive and Honey-Caramelized Carrots

This recipe by the Inn's chef de cuisine, Stacy Johnston, and Minette Lotz makes the most of late summer's pears and carrots, but it would also be delicious with the first apricots of late spring or the peaches of high summer. SERVES 4

Creek & Gully
Century Cider

CARROTS

5 to 6 farm-fresh carrots, cut into wedges

3 Tbsp local honey

1 tsp olive oil

Salt and black pepper, to taste

POACHED PEARS

2 sprigs thyme

2 bay leaves

2 Tbsp sugar

1 Tbsp black peppercorns

1½ cups red wine (from the Naramata Bench, of course!)

4 Bartlett or Anjou pears, peeled and quartered lengthwise (do not remove cores)

BLUE CHEESE CREAM

7 oz soft blue cheese (preferably Poplar Grove Tiger Blue)

½ cup whipping (33%) cream

Salt and black pepper, to taste

SALAD

3 to 5 endives, leaves separated and rinsed well

½ cup white wine vinegar

3 Tbsp honey

2 Tbsp Dijon mustard

¼ tsp thyme leaves

½ cup grapeseed oil

Salt and black pepper, to taste

½ cup toasted walnuts, for garnish

CARROTS Preheat oven to 425°F. Line a baking sheet with parchment paper.

Bring a medium saucepan of heavily salted water to a boil. Prepare a bowl of ice water.

Add carrots to the pan and cook for 4 to 5 minutes, until a fork just goes through the carrots and they are still a little firm. Drain carrots, then place them in the bowl of ice water to cool.

Drain carrots and transfer to a large bowl. Toss with honey, oil, salt and pepper. Spread out on the prepared baking sheet and roast for 15 minutes, until carrots are caramelized. Set aside to cool.

POACHED PEARS In a small saucepan, combine all ingredients, except pears, and bring to a simmer. Add pears and cover with a lid or parchment paper, ensuring the pears are completely submerged. Simmer for 10 to 15 minutes, until pears can be easily pierced with a knife.

Using a slotted spoon, transfer pears to a wire rack to cool. When pears are cool enough to handle, carefully cut out cores. (Poaching liquid can be reserved for future dishes and refrigerated for up to 1 month.)

BLUE CHEESE CREAM Put blue cheese in a bowl and whisk to break it up. Add cream and whip until thoroughly mixed. Season to taste with salt and pepper.

SALAD Set endive leaves on paper towels to dry.

Combine vinegar, honey, mustard and thyme in a blender and blend well. With the motor still running, gradually add oil and blend until emulsified. Season with salt and pepper.

ASSEMBLY Dollop blue cheese cream on 4 plates. Toss endive leaves in the dressing and arrange on the plates. Top with carrots, poached pears and toasted walnuts.

Arctic Char with Apple Jam and Hakurei Turnips

At the Naramata Inn, executive chef Ned Bell ensures that everything is sourced as locally (and ethically) as possible, and this dish is a good example. The apples, honey and turnips all come from Naramata farmers. Even the fish is farmed locally, by Bell's friend Gary Klassen and his family, in the middle of an apple orchard near Oliver. As Bell says: "You can only have this dinner here at Naramata Inn." Now you can bring that meal to your own house. SERVES 4

APPLE JAM

1 to 2 lbs apples (preferably Creek & Gully), peeled, cored and diced

1 tsp salt

½ cup honey (preferably Desert Flower Honey)

½ cup Creek & Gully apple cider

VINAIGRETTE

1 cup canola oil

½ cup apple cider vinegar

2 Tbsp Dijon mustard

2 Tbsp honey

1 tsp sea salt

1 tsp sumac (see Note)

APPLE JAM Combine all ingredients in a medium saucepan and simmer over medium-low heat for 20 minutes, until thick and jammy. Set aside to cool.

Apple jam can be stored in an airtight container in the fridge for 2 weeks. "It is a wonderful preserve for cheese, cheesecake and mild fish," says chef Ned Bell.

VINAIGRETTE Combine all ingredients in a Mason jar, cover and shake until well mixed.

NOTE Sumac has a sour, tangy citrus-like flavour that replaces lemons and limes on their all-local-ingredient menu. Although the chefs at Naramata Inn forage their own from the wilds of Naramata, you can purchase sumac at most grocery stores.

HAKUREI TURNIPS, THREE WAYS

2 lbs Hakurei turnips, peeled, stems reserved (divided)

½ onion, sliced

1 cup milk

1 cup heavy (36%) cream

1 bay leaf

Sea salt, to taste

1 Tbsp canola oil

Pinch of sumac

1 Tbsp butter

ASSEMBLY

2 to 4 Tbsp canola oil

4 (4- to 5-oz) portions Road 17 arctic char, wild B.C. salmon or responsibly farmed steelhead

Sea salt, to taste

1 apple, thinly shaved

HAKUREI TURNIPS, THREE WAYS For the turnip purée, combine ½ lb turnips with the onions, milk, cream and bay leaf in a large saucepan. Cover and simmer over medium heat for 20 minutes, until turnips are tender. Drain, reserving the cooking liquid. Discard bay leaf.

Add turnips to a blender, pour in ¼ to ½ cup of the cooking liquid and purée until smooth. The purée should be thicker than a soup and slightly thinner than mashed potatoes. Add more reserved cooking liquid if needed. Season to taste with sea salt.

For roasted turnips, preheat oven to 400°F. Line a baking sheet with parchment paper.

Peel and halve or quarter the remaining turnips, depending on the size. (They should be bite-sized.) Toss with just enough oil to lightly coat. Add a pinch of sea salt and sumac. Roast for 25 minutes, until golden brown and tender.

For sautéed turnip greens, rinse greens thoroughly and slice, if desired. Melt butter in a frying pan over medium heat. Add greens and sauté for 2 to 3 minutes, just until wilted. Do not overcook. Season with sea salt.

ASSEMBLY Heat oil in a frying pan over medium heat. Season fish with salt, then add to pan. Pan-sear for 2 minutes, then flip and cook for another 2 to 3 minutes.

To serve, swipe a few tablespoons of turnip purée onto each plate. Arrange a few roasted turnips and sautéed turnip greens around the purée. Place fish portions on each plate, then top with a tablespoon of apple jam and drizzle a healthy portion of vinaigrette overtop. Garnish with apple shavings.

NEVERLAND TEA COTTAGE

Renee Iaci, Gordon Kuang and Terri Tatchell
NARAMATA

The village of Naramata is a magical fairyland hidden away at the end of a winding road. It's not the sort of place you stumble upon by accident, but when you do, you might find your life changed forever.

Just ask Terri Tatchell. She's the Academy Award–nominated co-writer of *District 9* and the co-founder, with her childhood friend Renee Iaci (Shameless Hussy Productions), of Vancouver's Neverland Tea Salon. The Kitsilano tea room opened in 2013 as a celebration of decadence, whimsy and excellent bite-sized food.

Not long after that, chef Gordon Kuang, who was working for a catering company at the time, found himself in Neverland and met Tatchell for the first time. "I'd never had high tea before," he says. "I was hesitant because it was completely different from what I was used to. I'd always worked in kitchen-kitchens before."

Then COVID-19 came along. And like so many others, Tatchell was drawn outside the city and eventually bought a cottage in Naramata. In 2021, she opened it as a tea cottage surrounded by a storybook garden and invited Kuang to design the menu with the help of pastry chef Heather Jefferys.

Expect to find all the traditional finger sandwiches, scones, tartlets and other treats (with plenty of selection for gluten-free, vegan and other restrictive diets) and eighty types of tea. Kuang even infuses tea into some of the dishes, like the carrots he smokes with lapsang souchong to transform them into carrot lox. "It is like working in a chemistry lab with food," he says.

Still, he notes, "Scones are our most popular, and scones are the first recipe we ever tested. Our scones have been perfected."

Berry Pecan Salad with Neverland Apple Crumble Tea-Infused Raspberry Vinaigrette

Tea in your salad? Absolutely, says Neverland Tea Cottage executive chef Gordon Kuang. This fresh leafy green salad is bursting with berries and gets additional crunch from candied pecans and layers of fruity flavour from the dressing. SERVES 4

Elephant Island Winery
Crab Apple Wine

CANDIED PECANS
1 cup pecans
½ cup brown sugar
¼ tsp ground cinnamon
Pinch of salt
2 Tbsp water

VINAIGRETTE
2 cups raspberries
¾ cup brewed Neverland
   Tea Salon's Apple
   Crumble tea
⅓ cup apple cider vinegar
⅓ cup canola oil
⅔ cup extra-virgin olive oil

ASSEMBLY
10 cups Arcadian or
   spring lettuce mix
½ cup strawberries,
   quartered
½ cup blueberries
½ cup raspberries
½ cup blackberries
⅓ cup crumbled feta cheese

CANDIED PECANS Line a baking sheet with parchment paper.

Toast pecans in a small saucepan over medium heat for 2 to 3 minutes, stirring frequently. Transfer to the prepared baking sheet and spread out to cool.

In the same saucepan, combine brown sugar, cinnamon, salt and water. Stir until sugar is fully dissolved and bubbling. Return pecans to the saucepan and stir until nuts are fully coated. Cook for another 3 minutes, stirring frequently to prevent sugar from burning. Transfer nuts back to the prepared baking sheet, spreading them out in a single layer. Set aside to cool.

VINAIGRETTE Purée raspberries in a blender. Add the brewed tea and vinegar and blend again. With the blender still running, gradually add both oils and blend until emulsified.

Dressing can be stored in an airtight container in the fridge for up to 1 week.

ASSEMBLY Pat lettuce and berries dry, then place in a serving bowl. Add the desired amount of dressing and toss to coat. Top with feta and candied pecans. Serve immediately.

Vegan Blueberry Almond Joy Teacakes

These lovely little cakes, created by Neverland's chef Gordon Kuang, make a perfect afternoon snack. Note that both the batter and the glaze incorporate Neverland's tea; if you are unable to swing by the tea cottage, you can always order it online. MAKES 10 TEACAKES

TEACAKES DRY MIX

3⅓ cups almond meal
¾ cup flour
⅔ cup packed brown sugar
⅓ cup cornstarch
1 Tbsp finely ground Neverland Tea Salon's Almond Joy tea leaves
2 tsp baking powder
Pinch of salt

TEACAKES WET MIX

½ cup almond milk
½ cup melted coconut oil
½ tsp almond extract
½ cup blueberries

ALMOND JOY GLAZE

2½ cups icing sugar
½ cup brewed Neverland Tea Salon Almond Joy tea

OPTIONAL GARNISHES

Sliced blueberries
Edible flowers

TEACAKES Preheat oven to 350°F.

Sift dry mix ingredients into a large bowl.

Mix together wet mix ingredients, except blueberries. Fold dry ingredients into wet mix until fully incorporated. Gently stir in blueberries.

Transfer batter into 1- x 3-inch silicone moulds or a lightly sprayed muffin tin. Bake for 12 minutes, or until golden on top and a toothpick inserted into the centre of the teacakes comes out clean.

ALMOND JOY GLAZE In a small bowl, combine icing sugar and brewed tea and mix well. Drizzle over the teacakes. If desired, garnish with sliced blueberries and edible flowers.

THE NOBLE PIG BREWHOUSE

Maeghan and Jared Summers
KAMLOOPS

"I had a sense that this was going to be the new version of the neighbourhood pub," says Maeghan Summers, who co-owns The Noble Pig with her husband and chef Jared and their business partners. "We are focused on bringing community together, including the farmers and other suppliers."

When the Pig opened in 2010, it was the first brew pub in Kamloops and Maeghan and Jared were still living in Canmore and working at the Lodge at Kananaskis. One day while driving through Kamloops, they stopped into the Pig for lunch "and it turned into an interview," says Jared. Then it became a career change and a partnership that fundamentally changed a city. "Kamloops now has five craft breweries," Maeghan says. "And we're not competing, we're supporting each other."

Their first task was to change perceptions about beer. "We had to name our IPA 'The Pursuit of Hoppiness' because people wouldn't drink it if it was too hoppy," Maeghan says with a laugh. Their second was to connect with local producers. Now they work with twenty-three local suppliers of everything from beef to honey. "We're very much forging the way in Kamloops," she says.

Their second restaurant, called Underbelly, offers the kind of complex, multi-step dishes they can't manage at the high-volume Pig—where, Maeghan says, "The kitchen is so tiny it's like doing a ballet in a phone booth."

"Underbelly is another version of the Pig, but it's where we're doing all these crazy creative things. It's the Underbelly of the Pig."

Meanwhile, they've watched the city they love evolve, with the near-empty downtown coming alive with new businesses and residents attracted by what The Noble Pig started. As Maeghan says, "Community supporting community is critical to what we do."

Pickle Fried Chicken

At The Noble Pig, chef Jared Summers is always looking for ways to reduce waste and make produce go further. Here, he found a use for the pickle brine that would otherwise just go down the drain. "We've tried all sorts of fried chicken dishes over the years," he says. "This one has had an amazing response." SERVES 4 TO 8

Noble Pig
Big Bad Wolf IPA
or Papa G's ESB Bitter

QUICK-PICKLED CUCUMBERS

2 cloves garlic, crushed
4 tsp sugar
1 Tbsp salt
1 Tbsp dried dill
1 tsp pickling spice
1 tsp caraway seeds
¼ tsp celery seeds
¼ tsp crushed red pepper
Pinch of ground turmeric
1⅓ cups water
⅔ cup white vinegar
1 English cucumber, thinly sliced diagonally

BRINED CHICKEN

2 lbs boneless, skinless chicken thighs
1½ cups ready-made or homemade Pickle Juice (see here)

MARINADE

2 Tbsp coarse salt or 1½ Tbsp fine salt
2 Tbsp dried dill
2 Tbsp paprika
2 Tbsp poultry spice
1 Tbsp black pepper
2 tsp chili powder
1 tsp dry mustard
1 cup buttermilk
Brined Chicken (see here)

QUICK-PICKLED CUCUMBERS Combine all ingredients except the cucumbers in a saucepan. Gently simmer over medium heat, until salt and sugar are completely dissolved.

Place cucumbers in a clean 1-litre Mason jar (or two 500-mL jars). Immediately pour pickling liquid over the cucumbers. Cover jars with lids and tighten loosely. (The heat creates a vacuum that helps preserve the pickles and keeps them crisp.) Cool at room temperature, then refrigerate overnight. Makes about 4 cups, including 2 cups pickle juice.

As the pickles are not fully processed, they are not shelf stable. They can be refrigerated for 2 weeks.

BRINED CHICKEN Combine chicken and pickle juice. Cover and refrigerate for 3 hours.

MARINADE Meanwhile, combine all herbs and spices in a large bowl and mix well. Reserve 2 tablespoons for seasoning the finished chicken. Add buttermilk and stir to mix. Set aside.

Drain chicken thighs, then add to the marinade and mix well. Cover and refrigerate for at least 1 hour or overnight.

SPICY GARLIC MAYONNAISE

1 cup mayonnaise

1 tsp Sriracha, sambal oelek (Indonesian chili paste) or your favourite chili sauce

Grated zest and juice of 1 lime

1 clove garlic, grated

HOT HONEY

1 bay leaf

1 small cinnamon stick or ¼ tsp ground cinnamon

1 tsp crushed red pepper

½ tsp Sriracha, sambal oelek (Indonesian chili paste) or your favourite chili sauce

Grated zest of 1 orange

1 cup honey

ASSEMBLY

4 to 6 cups canola oil, for deep-frying

1 cup cornstarch

1 cup potato starch

1 cup rice flour

Hot Honey (see here)

2 Tbsp reserved spice blend from marinade

Spicy Garlic Mayonnaise (see here), to serve

16 slices Quick-Pickled Cucumbers (see here), to serve

1 lemon, cut into wedges, to serve

Greens, for garnish (optional)

SPICY GARLIC MAYONNAISE Combine all ingredients in a small bowl and mix well. Refrigerate for at least 1 hour or overnight. Makes 1 cup.

Spicy garlic mayonnaise can be stored in an airtight container in the fridge for 2 weeks.

HOT HONEY Combine all ingredients in a medium saucepan and bring to a gentle simmer over medium heat. Turn off heat and let steep for 1 hour. Strain through a fine-mesh sieve, then transfer to a clean container. Set aside to cool. Makes 1 cup.

Hot honey can be stored at room temperature for 1 month.

ASSEMBLY Pour oil into a deep fryer or deep saucepan and heat to a temperature of 265°F. Set a wire cooling rack over a baking sheet.

Combine cornstarch, potato starch and rice flour in a large bowl and mix well. Coat individual pieces of the marinated chicken in the dredging mixture. Working in small batches, gently fry chicken for 7 to 9 minutes, until the internal temperature of the chicken reaches 165°F. Transfer chicken to the rack to drain.

Increase heat of oil to 350°F. Carefully lower chicken into pan, in batches, taking care not to splash hot oil. Deep-fry for 2 minutes, until slightly brown. Remove from oil, then add chicken to hot honey and toss well. Repeat with remaining batches. Sprinkle with the reserved spice blend.

Serve with spicy garlic mayonnaise, quick-pickled cucumbers, lemon wedges and, if you like, some greens for garnish.

Ponzu Steak Salad

At Underbelly, this salad is not just delicious, it's also practical—it's a tasty way to use up all the steak trimmings that would otherwise be discarded. With the Asian flavours and candied jalapeños, it's perfectly beer-friendly and palate pleasing. As chef Jared Summers says, "It's been an absolute surprise hit on the menu." SERVES 4

> Noble Pig Straw House
> Munich Helles Lager

PONZU BEEF

1 cup tamari or soy sauce

2 Tbsp brown sugar

3 to 4 cloves garlic, chopped

1 (3-inch) piece ginger, peeled and chopped

1 to 2 tsp crushed red pepper

2 Tbsp lemon juice

2 Tbsp lime juice

2 Tbsp maple syrup

2 Tbsp neutral oil, such as canola oil

2 Tbsp sesame oil

1 lb beef striploin, trimmed

CANDIED JALAPEÑOS

3 jalapeños, cut into ¼-inch slices

1 Tbsp cornstarch

1 Tbsp water

2 cups sugar

½ tsp coriander seeds

¼ tsp salt

Pinch of ground turmeric

Pinch of celery seeds

1 cup apple cider vinegar

2 tsp lime juice

PICKLED RED ONIONS

1 red onion, thinly sliced

2 cups red wine

1 tsp pickling spice

1 cup red wine vinegar

½ tsp salt

½ tsp sugar

PONZU BEEF Combine tamari (or soy sauce) and brown sugar in a saucepan and dissolve sugar over medium heat. Remove from heat. Stir in the remaining ingredients, except striploin.

Combine striploin and marinade in a vacuum-seal bag. Seal and sous vide at 145°F for 3 hours. Once cooked, submerge the bag in ice water to cool quickly. Remove striploin from the bag, then pat dry with a cloth. Chill in the fridge until ready to serve.

Alternatively, if you don't have a sous-vide circulator, combine striploin and marinade in a zip-top bag and allow to marinate in the fridge for at least 4 hours or overnight. Preheat oven to 275°F. Line a baking sheet with a wire rack. Remove beef from marinade and place on the rack, reserving the marinade for basting. Roast for about 1 hour, basting occasionally, until internal temperature reaches 140°F. Remove from oven and allow to cool completely, then refrigerate until needed.

CANDIED JALAPEÑOS Place jalapeños in a clean 500-mL Mason jar.

In a small bowl, combine cornstarch and water and mix well to create a slurry. Set aside.

Combine remaining ingredients in a non-reactive saucepan and bring to a simmer over medium heat. Add slurry and simmer for another 10 minutes. Carefully pour the hot mixture over jalapeños.

Cover and loosely tighten the lid. Allow to cool at room temperature, then transfer to the fridge overnight. As the pickles are not fully processed, they are not shelf stable. They can be refrigerated for 2 weeks.

PICKLED RED ONIONS Place onions in a 1-litre Mason jar. In a saucepan, combine wine and pickling spice. Bring to a boil, then reduce heat to medium-low and simmer for 15 to 20 minutes, until reduced by half. Add vinegar, salt and sugar, stirring until sugar and salt have fully dissolved. Set aside to cool at room temperature for 15 minutes.

SESAME-LIME DRESSING

1 to 2 cloves garlic, finely chopped

1 Tbsp grated ginger

½ tsp crushed red pepper

½ tsp salt

Grated zest and juice of 1 lime

⅓ cup lime juice

¼ cup honey

1½ Tbsp tamari or soy sauce

1 Tbsp rice vinegar

2 tsp fish sauce

½ tsp Dijon mustard

6 to 7 Tbsp sesame oil

ASSEMBLY

1 lb chilled Ponzu Beef (see here)

4 cups salad greens

½ cup to 1 cup Sesame-Lime Dressing (see here)

3 radishes, thinly sliced

½ English cucumber, thinly sliced

1 cup Pickled Red Onions (see here)

½ cup Candied Jalapeños (see here)

Cilantro leaves, for garnish (optional)

Toasted sesame seeds, for garnish (optional)

Strain pickling liquid, then pour over onions. Cover and loosely tighten the lid. Allow to cool to room temperature, then refrigerate overnight.

As the pickles are not fully processed, they are not shelf stable. They can be refrigerated for 2 weeks.

SESAME-LIME DRESSING Combine all ingredients, except sesame oil, in a deep bowl or container. Using an immersion blender, blend until smooth. Slowly stream in sesame oil. (Alternatively, whisk by hand.) Makes about 1½ cups.

Leftover dressing can be stored in the fridge for up to 3 days.

ASSEMBLY Thinly slice beef and divide between 4 bowls.

In a medium bowl, combine salad greens and ½ cup of sesame-lime dressing and gently toss. Add more dressing to taste if desired. Place on top of the shaved beef. Add radishes, cucumbers, pickled onions and candied jalapeños. Garnish with cilantro and sesame seeds (if using). Finish with a drizzle of dressing. Serve immediately.

OLD VINES RESTAURANT AT QUAILS' GATE

Roger Sleiman
WEST KELOWNA

Few chefs have made as much of an impact on dining in the Okanagan Valley as Roger Sleiman at Old Vines Restaurant. He not only set the standard for fine winery cuisine, but he has also long been a champion of local farmers and mentor to countless young cooks.

Yet he fell into cooking by accident.

Born in Beirut, Sleiman was ten when his family emigrated to Canada. After university, he worked in a city planning office before moving to Whistler to spend the winter skiing. Cooking, he discovered, was a great way to support his lifestyle. "I was having fun cooking, but I knew I had to get serious," he recalls. "And then I fell in love with the industry." He spent twelve years cooking in Whistler, until 2006, when he joined Quails' Gate as winery chef. He has never looked back.

He immediately connected with local farmers and proudly put their names on his menu. "We try not to overdo it by listing twenty farmers for every dish," Sleiman says, but he is clearly tickled that the producers are what the servers talk about most when they describe a dish. "It's a great way to support new farmers."

Most of all, his food is always designed to complement the wine. "We're lucky because we have so many varietals here, and we always try to pair dishes with them," he says.

He also credits the winery's owners, the Stewart family, who have been part of the community for more than a century and were among the first to embrace and encourage locally focused, farm-to-table culinary experiences. "There's always something new every year to look forward to. It's hard to move when you have the best job in the valley," he says. "You cherish the relationships you build over the years."

Grilled Summer Peach and Burrata Salad

The Okanagan Valley is famous for its peaches. One of the very best ways to serve them is lightly grilled, as chef Roger Sleiman does in this summery salad—the heat adds a hint of smoke and depth to the fruit's sweetness. He pairs the peaches with local burrata, but you could also use a fresh ricotta or other creamy cheese if you like. SERVES 4

Quails' Gate
Three Wolves
Vineyard Pinot Gris

HAZELNUT CRUMB
1 cup brioche crumbs, toasted
¼ cup toasted hazelnuts, crushed
2 tsp olive oil
Salt

VINAIGRETTE
1 large shallot, quartered
3 Tbsp apple cider vinegar
2 Tbsp lemon juice
1 tsp Dijon mustard
¼ cup packed mint leaves
¼ cup packed basil leaves
¼ cup olive oil
Salt and black pepper, to taste

PEACHES
4 ripe peaches, halved and pitted
Olive oil, for coating
8 thin slices dry-cured ham, such as prosciutto or schinkenspeck
2 balls burrata cheese (about 4 oz each)
3 radishes, very thinly sliced
Arugula leaves
Basil leaves
Mint leaves

HAZELNUT CRUMB In a bowl, combine all ingredients and mix well.

VINAIGRETTE In a blender, combine shallots, vinegar, lemon juice and mustard and pulse until combined. Add mint, basil, oil, salt and pepper and blend until smooth and bright green. Refrigerate until needed.

PEACHES Preheat grill over medium heat.
Lightly coat peaches in oil in a small bowl. Add to the grill, cut-side down, and grill for 2 to 3 minutes, until slightly charred and caramelized. Quarter and set aside.

Evenly distribute peaches and 2 slices of ham on each serving plate. Divide the balls of burrata in half, and, using a spoon, scoop the creamy contents onto each plate alongside the peaches and ham. Sprinkle hazelnut crumb gently over the peaches. Arrange radishes, arugula, basil and mint around the salad. Drizzle vinaigrette overtop.

Spring Salmon with Pommes Anna, Morels, Peas and Garden Sorrel Sauce

Old Vines chef Roger Sleiman is passionate about using local and seasonal ingredients, and this elegant dish is a perfect expression of spring flavours. Spring salmon, also known as chinook or king salmon, is a rich, full-flavoured fish that is perfectly complemented by the morels and asparagus. SERVES 4

Quails' Gate
Stewart Family
Reserve Pinot Noir

POMMES ANNA

2 lbs Yukon Gold or Kennebec potatoes, peeled
½ cup clarified butter
Salt and black pepper, to taste

SAUCE

1 Tbsp butter
1 tsp olive oil
2 cups morel mushrooms, halved if large, well washed and patted dry
4 stalks asparagus, trimmed and cut diagonally into 1-inch segments
¼ cup white wine
2 cups heavy (36%) cream
¾ cup fresh or frozen English peas
1 tsp lemon juice
Salt and black pepper, to taste

SALMON

4 (5-oz) salmon fillets
Salt and black pepper, to taste
1 Tbsp vegetable oil
1 Tbsp butter
½ lemon

ASSEMBLY

½ cup sorrel leaves, thinly sliced
Pea tips, for garnish

POMMES ANNA Preheat oven to 350°F. Line a baking sheet with parchment paper.

Using a mandoline, slice potatoes into thin rounds and place in a bowl. Add clarified butter, salt and pepper and mix until potatoes are well coated. If butter begins to solidify, place bowl near a warm stove to liquify it.

On the prepared baking sheet, shingle potato slices tightly in 4 pinwheels, about 5 inches in diameter, and in 2 layers each. Season with salt and pepper between each layer. Bake for 30 to 40 minutes, until cooked through and golden. Set aside. (The potatoes can be prepared in advance and reheated when you are ready to serve.)

SAUCE Place butter and oil in a non-stick frying pan over medium heat. Add morels and asparagus and sauté for 5 to 10 minutes, until softened. Using a slotted spoon, transfer to a plate.

Add wine to the same pan and simmer for 5 to 7 minutes over medium heat, until reduced by half. Add cream and simmer

for another 15 minutes, or until reduced by half. Return mushrooms and asparagus to the pan, then add peas and lemon juice. Cook for 2 to 3 minutes, until warmed through. Season with salt and pepper. Keep warm.

SALMON Preheat oven to 400°F. Pat salmon dry with a paper towel. If you wish, remove salmon skin. Season with salt and pepper.

Heat oil in a heavy-bottomed, oven-proof frying pan over medium heat. Place salmon in pan, top side down, and press lightly to ensure full flesh contact with the pan. Transfer to the oven and roast for 3 to 4 minutes, until it forms a golden crust.

Remove from oven, flip the fillets and return the pan to medium heat. Add butter to the pan and squeeze lemon juice over salmon. Spoon melted lemon butter over the fillets several times.

ASSEMBLY Place 1 pommes Anna on each plate. Spoon sauce mixture evenly around the potatoes. Place a salmon fillet in the centre of each potato pinwheel. Scatter sorrel over the sauce and garnish with pea tips. Serve.

POPLAR GROVE

Rob Ratcliffe and Michael Ziff
PENTICTON

Don't let the view distract you, though it's understandable if it does. Poplar Grove's panorama on Munson Mountain sweeps some 180 degrees from Okanagan Lake to Skaha Lake and McIntyre Bluff to the south. But look away from the scenery and you will see a coolly contemporary dining space, elegantly crafted wines and chef Rob Ratcliffe's beautifully plated food.

He calls his style of cooking "refined nostalgia" and, although it references his English background, he says it's all about foods Canadians can relate to. Food and beverage manager Michael Ziff compares it to the kind of cuisine Canadian travellers are used to finding on wine tours abroad. "We create those experiences here at the winery and memories just as satisfying as the European ones," he says.

Poplar Grove was one of the first five wineries on the Naramata Bench, established in 1993 and purchased in 2007 by Tony and Barb Holler. They've placed the restaurant in the steady hands of Ziff and Ratcliffe, who had previously worked together at Hawksworth in Vancouver. "We've taken it up a notch in Penticton," Ratcliffe says. "We've focused on regionality and seasonality."

Dinner might mean the grilled duck hearts that have become a surprise guest favourite, his signature beef tartare or the "hidden gem," cured *hiramasa* (yellowtail amberjack) with shaved foie gras—all of it designed to go with Poplar Grove's powerhouse wines.

"Ultimately, we are a winery and our focus is wine. Our wines are so conducive to pairing with Rob's cooking and adding to the guest experience," Ziff says. "That recognition of quality and Rob's creative menu attract people."

Caramel Pot de Crème with Caramelized Peaches, Frosted Almonds and Chantilly Cream

Poplar Grove Chardonnay

Stone fruit season is chef Rob Ratcliffe's favourite time of year in the Okanagan Valley. Here, he uses peaches to top a rich caramel custard, but you could replace them with nectarines or apricots if you prefer. Just look for freestone varieties, which are so much easier to pit. SERVES 8

CARAMEL POT DE CRÈME

1 cup milk
1 cup whipping (33%) cream
½ tsp vanilla extract
¼ cup sugar
¼ tsp salt
⅔ cup dulce de leche (see Note)
6 egg yolks

CARAMELIZED PEACHES

¼ cup sugar
2 freestone peaches, halved and pitted

FROSTED ALMONDS

1 cup blanched almonds
½ cup sugar
¼ cup water

CHANTILLY CREAM

1 cup whipping (33%) cream
1 tsp vanilla extract
2 Tbsp icing sugar

CARAMEL POT DE CRÈME Preheat oven to 225°F. Arrange 8 (4-ounce) ramekins in a roasting pan. Set aside.

In a medium saucepan, combine milk, cream, vanilla, sugar and salt. Warm over medium heat for 10 minutes, stirring occasionally, until steaming but not boiling. Whisk in dulce de leche.

Put egg yolks into a bowl and stir to combine. Working very slowly to temper the egg and to avoid scrambling it, pour mixture over egg yolk, a little bit at a time, and whisk together. Pass through a fine-mesh sieve.

Divide mixture between the prepared ramekins, filling each about three-quarters full. Add hot (but not boiling) water to the pan until it comes about halfway up the outsides of the ramekins to create a bain marie. Wrap pan tightly in aluminum foil. Bake for 40 to 45 minutes, until custards are just set and jiggly in the centre. Remove from oven and chill until needed.

CARAMELIZED PEACHES Heat a non-stick frying pan over medium heat.

Pour sugar on a plate. Place peaches, cut side down, in the sugar to coat and pan-fry on that side only for 2 to 3 minutes, until sugar has caramelized. Transfer to a plate to cool.

FROSTED ALMONDS Preheat oven to 350°F. Line a baking sheet with parchment paper.

Place almonds on a separate baking sheet and toast for 10 minutes, until golden and fragrant.

Combine sugar and water in a small frying pan. Bring to a boil, then simmer for 5 minutes, or until it's thick and syrupy but not so long that it starts to change colour. Add almonds and stir until the outsides are coated in crystalized sugar.

Transfer to the prepared baking sheet and spread out to cool.

CHANTILLY CREAM In a stand mixer fitted with the whisk attachment, combine cream, vanilla and icing sugar. Whisk for 5 minutes, or until soft peaks form.

ASSEMBLY Slice the peaches and arrange them on the pots de crème. Spoon or pipe Chantilly cream over the peaches, then top with frosted almonds.

NOTE You can purchase dulce de leche, but it's easy to make this luxurious caramel yourself. Remove the label from a 300-mL can of sweetened condensed milk. Lay it on its side in a deep saucepan of water—it should be covered to at least 1½ times the height of the can. Bring the water to a boil and simmer for 2 hours. Make sure the can is submerged in water at all times, replenishing as needed.

Using tongs, carefully remove the can from the water and run it under cold running water until it is cool. Open the can and you will find a soft, rich and deep golden-brown caramel. Refrigerate until needed.

Buttermilk Soda Bread and Cultured Butter

At Poplar Grove, chef Rob Ratcliffe and his team make their own Parker House rolls and other breads, and whip up their own butter, too. This homemade butter is rich, creamy and deep in flavour—plus, your guests will be so impressed! The key to making this easy, flavourful loaf is buttermilk. MAKES 1 LOAF

 Poplar Grove Syrah

CULTURED BUTTER AND BUTTERMILK

4 cups whipping (33%) cream
1 Tbsp live yogurt (see Note)

BUTTERMILK SODA BREAD

Butter, for greasing
1 cup soft wheat flour
⅓ cup rye flour
½ cup Graham flour
   or whole wheat flour
¼ cup chopped
   dried apricots
¼ cup raisins
3 Tbsp sunflower seeds
3 Tbsp chopped pistachios
2 Tbsp flax seeds
1 tsp baking soda
½ tsp salt
2 cups reserved Cultured
   Buttermilk (see here)
3 Tbsp fancy molasses

CULTURED BUTTER AND BUTTERMILK
In a clean bowl, mix cream and yogurt. Cover bowl with a cheesecloth and set aside at room temperature for 24 hours.

Put mixture in the fridge for 1 hour.

Transfer to the bowl of a stand mixer fitted with the whisk attachment. Whip on high speed until it splits.

Switch the whisk attachment to a paddle and reduce speed to low. Mix for 10 to 15 minutes, until cream turns into butter. Drain buttermilk and reserve for the bread recipe.

Return butter to mixer and repeat the process 4 times. Refrigerate until needed.

NOTE Live yogurt contains beneficial bacteria known as probiotics, which aid the digestive system and help improve the body's balance of natural bacteria. On the label, look for the terms "live cultures" or "active cultures."

BUTTERMILK SODA BREAD Preheat oven to 350°F. Grease a loaf pan.

Mix all ingredients in a large bowl. Transfer to the prepared loaf pan. Top loaf with parchment paper and wrap with aluminum foil. Bake for 1 hour, until a toothpick inserted into the centre comes out clean. (If it is still sticky, bake for another 10 minutes.) Set aside to cool slightly. Slice and serve with cultured butter.

THE RESTAURANT AT PHANTOM CREEK

Alessa Valdez

OLIVER

If there is one winery, and one restaurant, that everyone in the South Okanagan has been talking about the last few years, Phantom Creek is it. People are fascinated by the massive building with its remarkable artwork, the historic vineyards, the superstar winemakers and, above all, the powerfully refined cuisine chef Alessa Valdez brings to the table.

Valdez came to Oliver from Toronto in 2020, very much a fish out of water but delighted to escape a city still largely under pandemic lockdowns. "I'm still adapting," she says. "It's nice coming from the city with all its restrictions. I was frustrated and nearly fell out of love with cooking."

Right away she started connecting with local farmers, who brought their produce right to her door ("I never had that in Toronto," she says) and she planted a small vegetable garden of her own. "It became my Zen, my peaceful place. The freshly picked potatoes and tomatoes from the garden are the best I've ever had," she says.

Valdez describes the food at Phantom Creek as casual fine dining, but that doesn't capture the subtle complexities on each plate. Her signature tartare, for instance, comes with pickled shimeji, XO yolk caramel, mushroom dust and tendon chips. "I like to showcase my personality on the plate," she says.

Due to a series of events that affected the valley (COVID-19, labour shortages, wildfires), the winery only opened for limited hours in 2021 and had a delayed opening in 2022. Even so, Valdez says, "We did make a mark. We put the restaurant on the map. Now I want it to be the best restaurant in the Okanagan."

Phantom Creek Smoky Hemingway

Ernest Hemingway was known to like a cocktail or two, and Cooper Callaghan's riff on the famous daiquiri named in his honour combines the smoky flavour of mezcal with bittersweet grapefruit. Underpinning it all is the Marrow Vermouth made in Penticton by Shawn Dalton, who uses all-local ingredients in his aperitif-style wines. SERVES 1

GRAPEFRUIT CORDIAL

Zest and juice of
1 grapefruit (ideally ruby red)

An equal amount of sugar

SMOKY HEMINGWAY

1½ oz Montelobos Mezcal

½ oz Marrow Arancio Vermouth or your favourite sweet white vermouth

¾ oz Grapefruit Cordial (see here)

¼ oz lemon juice

Lemon rind, for garnish

GRAPEFRUIT CORDIAL Place juice and sugar into a non-reactive saucepan and cook over medium heat, stirring, until it reaches 185°F and sugar is dissolved. Remove from heat and stir in zest. Let sit at room temperature overnight, then strain.

SMOKY HEMINGWAY Shake all liquid ingredients with ice. Strain, then pour into a chilled Nick and Nora glass (or martini glass). Garnish with the lemon rind.

Duck Breast with Red Cabbage Purée, Seared Red Cabbage, Pickled Cherries and Miso-Red Wine Jus

Duck and red cabbage are a classic pairing, but here Alessa Valdez, executive chef at Phantom Creek Winery, elevates it to something new and exciting. "The dish itself is very complex in layers and flavours, but it all works so well together," Valdez says. "This is basically me on a plate." You will need to start curing the cabbage twenty-four hours before you prepare it. SERVES 4

 Phantom Creek Estates
Kobau Vineyard Syrah

SEARED RED CABBAGE

1 small head red cabbage
¼ cup salt
2 Tbsp sugar
½ tsp ground ginger
½ tsp ground allspice
½ tsp ground white pepper
½ tsp ground cloves
½ tsp ground cinnamon
Olive oil, for drizzling

PICKLED CHERRIES

120 g black cherries, pitted
    and halved (about ¾ cup)
¼ cup red wine vinegar, plus
    extra if needed

MISO–RED WINE JUS

1 Tbsp extra-virgin olive oil
1 small shallot, chopped
2 cloves garlic, finely
    chopped
2 Tbsp sugar
1¼ cups red wine
Sprig of thyme
Sprig of rosemary
1 bay leaf
1¼ cups chicken stock
3 Tbsp miso paste
Salt and black pepper,
    to taste
2 Tbsp butter

SEARED RED CABBAGE Cut red cabbage in half, then into quarters. (This keeps the cabbage core intact so it doesn't fall apart.)

In a small bowl, combine remaining ingredients, except oil, and mix well. Lightly season both sides of quartered cabbage with the spice blend, making sure to get in between each layer. Refrigerate for 24 hours on a wire rack to cure.

Preheat oven to 375°F. Rinse off excess seasoning and pat dry with a paper towel.

Heat a frying pan or a grill pan over high heat. Drizzle oil over cabbage quarters, then sear each side for 3 minutes. Transfer red cabbage to a baking sheet and cover with aluminum foil. Bake for 20 minutes, until tender. Keep warm until ready to serve.

PICKLED CHERRIES Meanwhile, place cherries and vinegar in a small bowl. Add extra vinegar, if needed, to cover. Set aside and allow to marinate for 30 minutes at room temperature.

MISO–RED WINE JUS Heat oil in a small saucepan over medium heat. Add shallots and sauté for 2 to 3 minutes, until softened and just beginning to colour. Add garlic and sauté for another minute, until fragrant.

Stir in sugar and cook for 1 minute, then pour in wine. Add thyme, rosemary and bay leaf. Bring to a boil and boil for 10 minutes, until wine is reduced by three-quarters and syrupy.

Pour in stock and bring to another boil. Boil for 5 to 10 minutes, until reduced by half. (It can be reduced further if you want a more concentrated sauce.) Whisk in miso paste.

Strain through a fine-mesh sieve and return to the pan. Heat through and season with salt and pepper. Whisk in butter. Keep warm.

RED CABBAGE PURÉE

2 Tbsp vegetable oil

2 shallots, thinly sliced

1 small head red cabbage, cored and julienned

½ cup red wine

2 cups water

½ cup red wine vinegar

1½ Tbsp Dijon mustard

2 tsp cold butter

2 tsp salt

DUCK

4 (6-oz) duck breasts

1 Tbsp salt

Flaky sea salt, such as Maldon, to serve

GARNISH (OPTIONAL)

4 leaves chicory, chopped

4 leaves mustard greens, chopped

Olive oil

Sea salt

RED CABBAGE PURÉE Heat oil in a medium saucepan over medium heat. Add shallots and sauté for 5 minutes, until translucent. Add cabbage and sauté for another 5 minutes, until softened.

Add wine and stir to deglaze pan. Cook for another 10 to 15 minutes, until reduced by half. Pour in water and vinegar and cover. Cook for 10 to 15 minutes, until cabbage is soft.

Drain cabbage, reserving liquid. Transfer cabbage to a high-powered blender or food processor and purée. Add mustard, butter and salt and purée again. (If purée seems too thick, thin out with the reserved liquid.) For a truly smooth purée, pass it through a fine-mesh sieve. Cool over an ice bath.

DUCK Using a sharp knife, gently score skin on duck breasts in a tight crosshatch pattern, spaced ⅛ inch apart. Season duck with salt, heavily on the skin side and lightly on the flesh side.

Place duck breasts, skin side down, in a large, cold frying pan. Heat pan over low to medium-low heat for 5 minutes, until fat begins to gently bubble. (If the fat is either silent or spitting, adjust heat accordingly.) Pour out rendered fat and pan-fry for 10 to 12 minutes, until skin is golden brown and the internal temperature reaches 125°F. (If needed, pan-fry for another minute to colour the skin.)

Flip and cook for another 1 to 2 minutes, until breasts register 130°F on an instant-read thermometer for rare. (Cook to 140°F for medium or 155°F for well-done.) Transfer duck to a cutting board and set aside to rest for 10 minutes.

ASSEMBLY Cut duck breast in half lengthwise and place on the left side of each plate. Season with flaky salt. Place cabbage purée next to the duck, then add seared red cabbage slightly overlapping the purée. Arrange pickled cherries evenly around the plates and drizzle miso–red wine jus in the centres. If using the garnish, combine chicory, mustard greens, oil and salt in a bowl and toss to coat. Add to plates and serve.

ROW FOURTEEN AT KLIPPERS ORGANICS

Derek Gray

CAWSTON

You have not tasted a tomato until you've tasted the tomato Derek Gray puts on your sandwich at Row Fourteen, the restaurant at Klippers Organics (page 92). It is so sweet, so intense, so utterly tomato-y, it's practically life changing.

Gray gets it. He first visited the farm owned by Kevin and Annamarie Klippenstein back when he was still the restaurant chef at Vancouver's Osteria Savio Volpe. "Cawston is beautiful. I couldn't believe I had never been there," he says. He recalls biting into a peach picked from the tree. "It was warm, juicy and so inviting," he says. That was the moment he decided, "A restaurant on a farm is the future for me."

He—alongside Kevin and Annamarie, a collaboration they called "one chef and two farmers"—opened Row Fourteen (located on the fourteenth row of the fruit orchard) on August 2, 2019. "We started off with a bang," he says. "We lucked out because we had Alexandra Gill come in." The *Globe and Mail* reviewer rated it Vancouver's best new restaurant that year, despite the four-hour drive from the city. But by the time the article ran, they were closed for winter and scheduled to reopen in March 2020. Then COVID-19 hit.

Through pandemic, fires, floods and everything else, Gray and his talented team have kept making food that is more flavourful than anything you've ever tasted, because it's been picked minutes before it hits your plate.

"The food is hyper-seasonal. When we look at the weeks to come, farmhands will be telling us broccolini is at its peak right now or cherry tomatoes are at their absolute peak," he says. "We focus on vegetables first and foremost because we're in the Similkameen, so we want to showcase what grows on the farm and in the valley."

He adds, "It's really simple, but that's our food. We're one-ingredient driven."

Smashed Peas on New Season's Potatoes

This is one of chef Derek Gray's favourite ways to enjoy the flavour of fresh English peas. The combination of virgin canola oil and aged cheddar makes this a refreshing bite, he says, and suggests serving with the first sweet, tender, buttery potatoes of the new season. "This simple recipe only calls for a pestle and mortar, a little arm work and some patience when shucking the peas," he says. SERVES 2

Untangled Craft Cider
Tangled Apple Cider

POTATOES IN BUTTER

1 lb small new potatoes, such as Warba or yellow German (see Note)

3 Tbsp butter

5 Tbsp water, plus extra if needed

Salt and black pepper, to taste

SMASHED PEAS

6 to 8 leaves fresh mint, plus extra for garnish

Pinch of salt, plus extra to taste

1 cup freshly shucked English peas (divided)

¼ cup grated two-year-old aged hard cheese, such as cheddar (divided), plus extra for garnish

2 Tbsp virgin cold-pressed canola oil (divided), plus extra as needed

White pepper, to taste

POTATOES IN BUTTER Place potatoes into a pot of cold, salted water and bring to a boil over medium-high heat. Reduce heat to medium-low and simmer for 15 minutes, until potatoes can be pierced without resistance. Drain.

Combine butter and water in the same saucepan over medium heat. Add potatoes and toss to coat well. Season with salt and pepper. It's okay if some of the potatoes break up—it will help develop the sauce.

NOTE Warba potatoes are an heirloom variety originally introduced in the 1920s. It was designed to be an early-producing crop (June to August) and several local farms grow them, including Klippers Organics.

SMASHED PEAS Using a mortar and pestle, grind mint and a pinch of salt to a paste. Add ½ cup peas and grind until they are broken up. Add half the cheese, half the remaining peas and a teaspoon or two of oil, then grind again. Repeat with the remaining cheese and peas, and another teaspoon or so of oil. (As the peas are being ground, the starch will be released and the fat in the cheese and oil will make the peas creamier.) Season with salt and pepper. (Alternatively, combine ingredients in a food processor and blitz until creamy. "But where is the fun in that?" Gray asks!) Serve immediately or the peas will quickly begin to brown.

Place buttered potatoes on plates. Cover with smashed peas. Garnish with mint, finely grated cheddar and a drizzle of oil.

Beets and Sake Kasu Whey

Chef Derek Gray recommends you begin any recipe by "shopping and supporting your local farmers' market or favourite farm. Good ingredients make great food." The roasted beet base of this recipe can be made year-round as beets store well, and the dish can be topped with fresh and seasonal fruit, such as the blackberries here. SERVES 2

 Untangled Craft Cider
Black Peach Cider

BEETS

2 beets, washed and scrubbed clean
2 cloves garlic
3 sprigs thyme
1 Tbsp olive oil, plus extra for drizzling
Pinch of salt
Pinch of black pepper
Aged red wine vinegar, to taste

WHEY

2 cups milk
2 cups buttermilk
¼ cup sake kasu (see Note)

ASSEMBLY

Flaky sea salt (such as Maldon) and black pepper, to taste
Handful of seasonal fruit, such as blackberries
Toasted nuts, such as hazelnuts, roughly chopped

BEETS Preheat oven to 400°F.

In a bowl, combine all ingredients, except vinegar, and toss well. Wrap beets and aromatics in aluminum foil and roast for 45 minutes to 1 hour, until a sharp paring knife can be inserted in the beets without any resistance. Unwrap beets and set aside to slightly cool.

Reduce oven heat to 250°F. Line a baking sheet with parchment paper.

Using a paring knife, peel beets and cut into bite-sized wedges. Place them on the prepared baking sheet and bake for 1 hour. (Alternatively, you could do as Gray does and toast them over an open fire to dehydrate the flesh slightly and intensify the flavour.)

Take the beets out of the oven and transfer them to a bowl. Add a pinch of salt and pepper, a dash of both red wine vinegar and oil, and mix to dress the beets. Set aside until needed.

WHEY Combine milk and buttermilk in a large saucepan. Warm over medium heat for 3 to 5 minutes, until milk begins to curdle. Strain liquid into another saucepan, reserving curds. Simmer for 20 to 40 minutes, stirring frequently, until reduced by half, thick and caramelized.

Add sake kasu, then reduce heat to low and cook for 5 minutes to develop flavour. Transfer mixture to a high-power blender and blend for 1 minute on high speed. If your sauce is too loose, blend in some of the curds to thicken. The consistency should be thick and creamy. Keep warm.

ASSEMBLY Transfer beets to a serving bowl. Cover with warm whey. Top with blackberries and finish with flaky salt and black pepper. Sprinkle with toasted nuts.

NOTE Sake kasu is the leftover lees from making sake. Chefs love using it as a marinade that adds umami-rich flavours to food. It is available from Japanese specialty stores including Artisan Sake-Maker in Vancouver.

SILVER STAR RESORT

Scott Sanderson and Anna Blixhavn

VERNON

Nothing whets the appetite quite like a day spent hiking, biking or skiing in the mountains, and SilverStar's executive chef Scott Sanderson is determined that no one will leave his mountain hungry. He oversees seven cafés, restaurants, pubs and lounges that turn out everything from grab-and-go granola bars to high-end yet casual sit-down dining.

He arrived here from Ontario, where he'd worked in an independent Italian restaurant for nine years, "dead set" on moving to Kelowna—until someone told him about Silver Star. "And seven years later, here I am," he says. "It's a magical village and a great community. It's a hidden gem."

He's assembled a strong core team, including talented pastry chef Anna Blixhavn, and extended the dining season year-round, especially at The Red Antler, a popular spot serving Canadian comfort food. The resort may be casual and easygoing, but the attention to ingredients and preparation is anything but.

"We make all our sauces in house. We make our own chicken parmigiana meatballs," Sanderson says. "We smoke our meats, ribs and pork butt. "Our café in Town Hall is all fresh in-house-baked pastries—cookies, muffins and different types of squares."

His team has also forged relationships with valley wineries and farms, including Silverstar Veggies just down the hill. "It's nice when you can drop a salad at a table and say, 'These greens were grown just twenty minutes down the road.'"

He credits a supportive food and beverage team and a supportive ownership—as well as a diverse clientele that includes plenty of families—for making his job so satisfying. "I'm fortunate," he says. "The village vibes are amazing. People are just getting out and enjoying themselves."

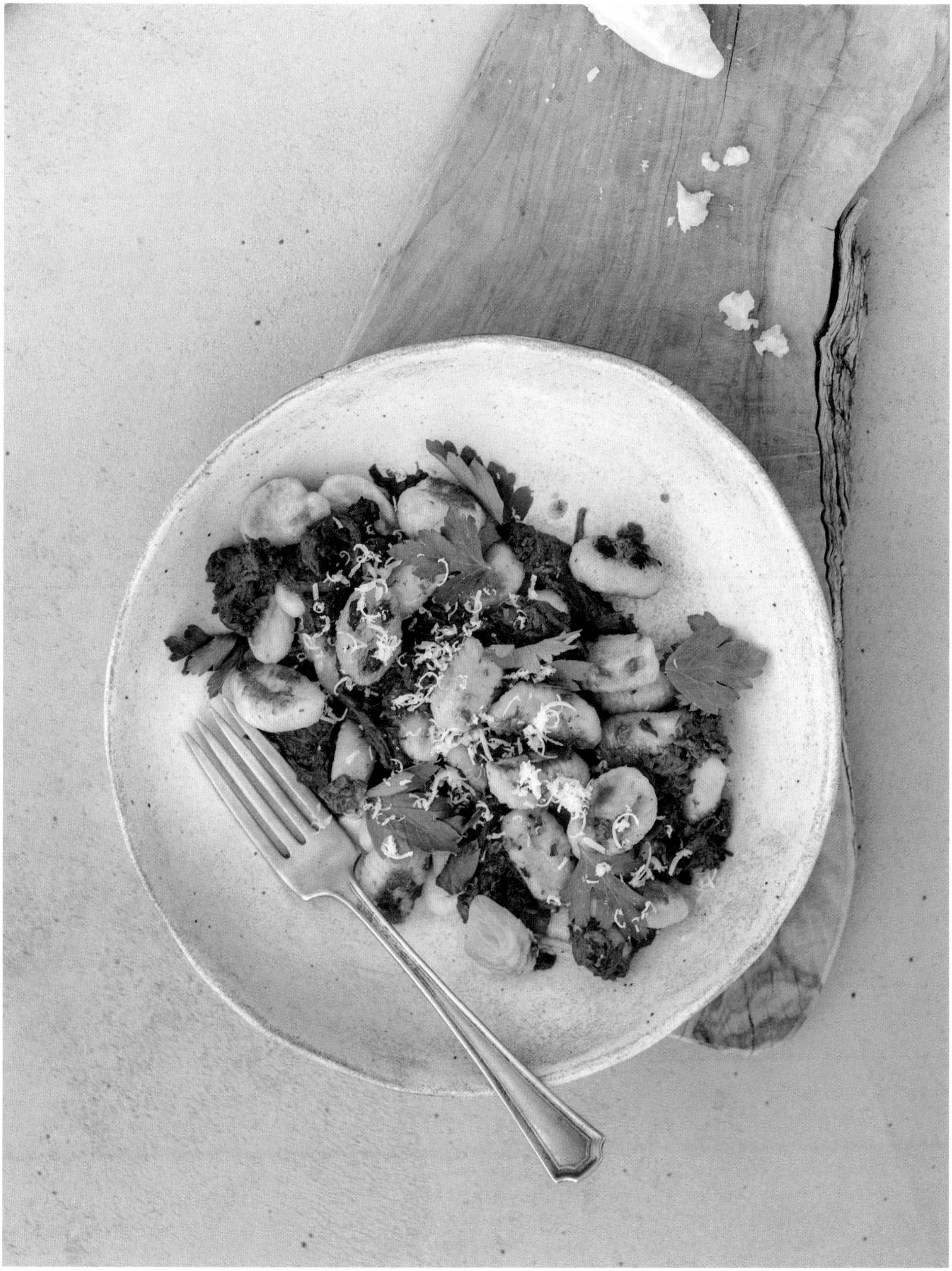

Potato Gnocchi with Venison Ragù, p. 147

Potato Gnocchi with Venison Ragù

Silver Star resort's executive chef Scott Sanderson spent years working at a popular Italian restaurant in Ontario, where he made dishes like this updated classic. It is the kind of hearty fare skiers and cyclists love after an action-packed day on the mountain and it's made even better with the addition of Okanagan Valley wine, especially a bold, well-structured Cabernet Franc. SERVES 4

Rust Wine Co.
Cabernet Franc

VENISON RAGÙ

1 (2- to 3-lb) boneless netted venison shoulder

6 cloves garlic, smashed

1 onion, chopped

½ carrot, chopped

½ stalk celery, chopped

2 Tbsp black peppercorns, crushed

1 Tbsp juniper berries

1 (750-mL) bottle Okanagan Cabernet Franc, such as Rust Wine Co.

1 to 2 Tbsp vegetable oil

Salt, as needed

GNOCCHI

Coarse salt, as needed

4 Yukon Gold potatoes (2½ lbs)

1¼ cups flour

1 Tbsp salt

Pinch of white pepper

½ tsp extra-virgin olive oil

1 free-range egg

Semolina flour, for dusting

ASSEMBLY

1 Tbsp olive oil

1 Tbsp butter

Shaved Grana Padano cheese

Italian parsley, chopped

VENISON RAGÙ The night before serving the dish, place venison in a large non-reactive bowl and add garlic, onions, carrots, celery, peppercorns, juniper berries and wine. Mix well. Allow to marinate in the fridge overnight.

The next day, preheat oven to 300°F. Remove venison from the marinade, reserving marinade for later.

Heat oil in a large cast-iron frying pan over medium-high heat. Pat venison dry, then generously season with salt. Add it to the pan and sear for 3 minutes on each side, or until browned. Transfer venison to a braising pan or Dutch oven at least 4 inches deep.

In a separate saucepan, bring the marinade to a boil so the flavours meld. Pour it over the venison. Cover with a lid or aluminum foil and braise for 6 hours. Set aside until cool enough to handle.

Reserving braising liquid, transfer venison to a cutting board and shred it. Season to taste with salt.

Bring braising liquid to a boil, then reduce heat and simmer for at least 20 minutes, until reduced by half. Add the shredded venison. (You can make the dish ahead of time to this point and reheat the ragù when you need it.)

GNOCCHI Preheat oven to 400°F. Line a baking sheet with a layer of coarse salt.

Using a fork, pierce potatoes to allow steam to escape. Bake for 1 hour, until fork tender. Set aside until cool enough to handle.

Peel off potato skins. Using a potato ricer, rice potatoes. (You'll have about 1 lb of fluffy potatoes.) Place riced potatoes in a large bowl, then add flour, salt, pepper, oil and egg. Gently mix together, then turn out onto a work surface dusted with semolina flour. Knead until a dough forms. Wrap in plastic wrap and let rest in the fridge for 30 to 45 minutes.

Dust a baking sheet with semolina flour. Divide dough into 4 equal pieces. Using your hands, roll each piece into an even log, about 1 inch in diameter. Cut each rope of dough into ½-inch pieces.

Use your thumb to roll each piece of gnocchi along the tines of a fork, to create a lined pattern. (Or use a wooden gnocchi board.) Place on the prepared baking sheet, cover with plastic wrap and refrigerate until needed.

ASSEMBLY Bring a large saucepan of salted water to a boil. Drop gnocchi into the water and cook for 1 to 2 minutes, until they float to the surface.

Meanwhile, heat oil and butter in a large, non-stick frying pan over medium heat. Using a slotted spoon, transfer gnocchi to the pan and cook for 5 to 10 minutes, until lightly golden brown.

Transfer to a large serving platter or divide among 4 plates. Top with warm venison ragù, shaved Grana Padano and a generous sprinkle of parsley.

Okanagan Fruit Clafoutis with Red Wine Ice Cream

Clafoutis is a classic French dish, somewhere between a pancake and baked custard and stuffed with fresh fruit. At SilverStar Mountain Resort, pastry chef Anna Blixhavn uses in-season Okanagan fruit but her favourites are local cherries or huckleberries. The red wine ice cream, of course, makes the most of the valley's other famous product. SERVES 4

Okanagan Spirits
Cherry Liqueur
or Kirsch Danube

RED WINE ICE CREAM

1 (750-mL) bottle red wine, such as Ex Nihilo Merlot

⅔ cup brown sugar

2 cups heavy (36%) cream

4 egg yolks

1 vanilla bean, split lengthwise and seeds scraped, or 1 tsp vanilla extract

1 cup half-and-half

CLAFOUTIS

3 Tbsp butter, melted and room temperature, plus extra for greasing

½ cup flour

½ cup sugar

Pinch of salt

3 eggs

¼ tsp vanilla extract

Grated zest of 1 lemon

1 cup milk

2 cups berries or fruit of your choice, such as Okanagan cherries or huckleberries

Icing sugar, for dusting

Red Wine Ice Cream (see here), to serve

RED WINE ICE CREAM Pour wine into a saucepan. Gently simmer over medium-low heat, stirring frequently, until reduced to 1 cup. Keep a close eye on the pan—it will take at least 15 minutes and possibly up to 45.

In a separate saucepan, combine sugar and cream and bring to a scald over medium heat. (The sugar will dissolve and the cream will steam and have bubbles at the edges.)

In a bowl, whisk egg yolks and vanilla seeds (or extract). Very slowly pour the hot cream mixture into the eggs, whisking constantly and taking care not to cook the yolks. Pour back into the pan and cook over low heat. Stir constantly, scraping the bottom of the pan to prevent any bits from sticking, until mixture is thick enough to coat the back of a spoon and the temperature reaches 185°C. (Cooking slowly and stirring frequently prevents it from curdling.)

Remove from heat. Strain mixture through a fine-mesh sieve into a clean bowl. Stir in reduced wine and half-and-half.

Cover bowl, then refrigerate for at least 2 hours or overnight. Pour cooled mixture into an ice cream maker and freeze according to the manufacturer's instructions.

CLAFOUTIS Preheat oven to 350°F. Grease a 9-inch glass pie pan, gratin dish or round casserole.

In a bowl or blender, combine flour, sugar, salt, eggs, melted butter, vanilla and lemon zest and blend until smooth. Add milk and whisk for 3 minutes, until light and smooth.

Pour batter into the dish and top with berries (or other fruit). Bake for 30 to 50 minutes, until clafoutis is set, golden and puffed up in the centre and a skewer inserted into the centre comes out clean. Set aside to cool slightly. The custard might still be jiggly when removed from the oven, and it will likely deflate as it cools.

Dust with icing sugar, cut into wedges and serve warm with ice cream.

SMALL AXE ROADHOUSE

Sarah Dudley
ENDERBY

With a population a smidge under 3,000 and just one main street, Enderby is about as small as a city can get. But that suits Sarah Dudley just fine. She'd been working in Vancouver pubs as well as "a fancy tweezered-food bistro" in Whistler, and says, "I just wasn't feeling the city anymore after thirteen years."

Then she found the Small Axe Roadhouse. The couple who had opened it in 2017 were ready to move on, and she took ownership in 2019. She painted the walls turquoise and crammed the place with artwork, "a billion" record album covers and neon signs. "It's cosy and rustic," Dudley says, admitting, "I love neon signs so much. I have a problem."

She describes it as "a dive bar with surprisingly delicious comfort food and crafty cocktails. . . all, of course, made with love, by weirdos." No wonder her regulars are happy to drive the thirty minutes from Salmon Arm and Vernon for the ground chuck smash burgers and Big Ole Yorkie Bowl (page 151), the dozen beers on tap and the fun atmosphere. "That makes you feel great," she says.

With Enderby being right on the border between the North Okanagan and the Shuswap, Sarah is surrounded by growers and producers and she does her best to support local farmers—for instance, by hosting what she calls "Farmers' Market Fridays." "We want to be fun and inclusive. People were hungry for a place where the food is different. We came in and did pretty good food and people appreciate that," she says. "I'm super proud. I finally own my own place and I've got a good crew, and they're helping me live the dream. We're a big dysfunctional yet functioning family first."

Big Ole Yorkie Bowl

How hungry are y'all? This Small Axe Roadhouse dish is hearty, soul-satisfying and fun, too. Don't be intimidated by the idea of Yorkshire puddings—they are so easy to make, says owner Sarah Dudley. "The secret is in the fat you cook 'em in," she says. "I prefer beef fat or pork lard, but vegetable shortening works, too." You will need gratin dishes, and it will take about three hours for the brisket to braise before you make the Yorkies. SERVES 8

 Crannóg Ales Back Hand of God Stout

BRISKET

5 to 6 lbs beef brisket

4 carrots, chopped into 1-inch dice

4 stalks celery, chopped into 1-inch dice

2 onions, chopped into 1-inch dice

4 to 6 cloves garlic

2 Tbsp vegetable oil

Salt and black pepper, to taste

1 cup red wine

3 bay leaves

3½ litres beef stock

3 to 4 Tbsp flour or cornstarch (optional)

YORKIE BOWLS

10 eggs (about 2 cups)

2 cups flour

1 tsp salt

2 cups milk

½ cup fat or shortening

Mashed potatoes, to serve (optional)

2 Tbsp horseradish, to serve (optional)

½ cup sour cream, to serve (optional)

BRISKET Preheat oven to 350°F. (See Note.)

Trim brisket, leaving as much of the fat cap on as you like. Cut into 2-inch cubes. Place brisket in a roasting pan, then add carrots, celery, onions and garlic. Drizzle oil on top, then season with salt and pepper. Mix well. Roast for 20 to 25 minutes, stirring 2 to 3 times, until evenly browned.

Remove pan from oven, then reduce heat to 325°F. Add wine to deglaze the pan, scraping up any browned bits from the bottom. Add bay leaves and pour in enough stock to generously cover beef and veggies. Cover with aluminum foil and make sure to completely seal. Bake for 2 to 2½ hours, until meat is very tender.

To thicken gravy, whisk in flour (or cornstarch) if you like. Set aside and keep warm.

YORKIE BOWLS In a large bowl, whisk together eggs, flour, salt and milk. Set aside on your work surface for 20 minutes. Do not refrigerate.

Preheat oven to 450°F. Arrange 8 individual gratin dishes on a baking sheet. (This makes it easier to transfer them in and out of the oven.)

Put a tablespoon of fat (or shortening) in each dish and heat in the oven for 8 minutes.

Take bowls out of the oven. Working quickly and carefully, use a 6-oz ladle to ladle batter into the hot fat (or oil). Return to oven and reduce heat to 400°F. Bake for 7 minutes.

Reduce heat to 350°F and bake for another 7 minutes, until Yorkies are puffed high and golden brown.

ASSEMBLY Place a layer of mashed potatoes (if using) into the Yorkie bowls, then top with brisket along with a generous amount of gravy.

In a small bowl, combine horseradish and sour cream (if using) and serve with the Yorkie bowls.

NOTE Cooking temperatures and times indicated in this recipe are for a convection oven, which circulates air, making for faster, more even heating. If you are using a conventional oven, you may need to cook the dishes a few minutes longer and may even want to turn the heat up by 25°F.

Benny Crabitz with Potato Latkes

At Small Axe Roadhouse, owner Sarah Dudley serves these savoury crab cakes at brunch in a dish she calls "crab Bennies with fancy-ass potato cakes." You can do the same or serve them on their own with just a squeeze of lemon and a Lenny Kravitz playlist. SERVES 6 TO 8

Upside Cider
Harvest Apple Cider

DEEP-DISH POTATO LATKES

Non-stick cooking spray
8 Kennebec or russet potatoes, unpeeled, washed and then shredded (8 cups)
3 cloves garlic
1 onion, finely chopped
1 cup shredded cheese of your choice
1 Tbsp garlic powder
2 Tbsp onion powder
2 tsp salt
2 tsp black pepper
½ cup sour cream
6 eggs
Oil, for frying (optional)

BENNY CRABITZ

¼ cup (½ stick) butter
1 red bell pepper, seeded, deveined and finely chopped
1 yellow onion, finely chopped
3 cloves garlic, finely chopped
2 lbs fresh crabmeat, picked of shells or cartilage
3 eggs
Small bunch of green onions, thinly sliced
1½ cups panko crumbs
2 tsp seasoning salt
1½ tsp black pepper
Grated zest and juice of 2 lemons
½ cup mayonnaise

ASSEMBLY

1 cup flour
4 eggs, lightly beaten
1½ cups panko crumbs
2 to 4 Tbsp vegetable oil
Toasted English muffins, poached eggs, hollandaise sauce, capers and/or thinly sliced red onions, to serve (optional)

DEEP-DISH POTATO LATKES Preheat oven to 350°F. Spray a deep 9- x 13-inch baking dish with cooking spray and line it with parchment paper.

Combine the remaining ingredients, except the oil, in a large bowl. Transfer to the prepared baking dish and press in gently. Cover with aluminum foil and bake for 30 to 45 minutes, until cooked through.

Remove foil and bake for another 5 to 10 minutes, until golden brown. Set aside to cool.

Cut into 8 squares. Serve as is, or fry them until they are crisp on all sides. "They are bonkers good this way," Dudley says.

BENNY CRABITZ Melt butter in a frying pan over low heat. Add bell peppers, onions and garlic and sauté for 5 to 8 minutes, until softened and semi-translucent. Set aside to cool.

Squeeze excess juice from crabmeat. In a large bowl, combine crabmeat, eggs, green onions, panko, salt, pepper, lemon juice and zest, and mayo. Gently mix in onion–bell pepper mixture. Refrigerate for 1 to 2 hours, until set. You don't want it too sticky or too dry.

ASSEMBLY Shape mixture into 16 compact balls and flatten slightly, being sure to keep them tightly packed so they don't fall apart during cooking. Put flour into a shallow bowl. Whisk eggs in another. Place panko in a third. Dip each crab cake into flour, egg and then panko. Heat oil in a frying pan over medium heat. Working in batches to avoid overcrowding, add crab cakes and pan-fry for 2 to 3 minutes. Turn and cook for another 2 minutes, or until crisp and golden brown.

Serve the crab cakes on top of the deep-dish potato latkes, or with the latkes on top of English muffins and topped with your favourite hollandaise sauce and Benny accompaniments.

SPARKLING HILL RESORT

John Stratton
VERNON

Sparkling Hill Resort is a gem of the North Okanagan, with millions of Swarovski crystals glittering throughout the property, an exceptional European-style spa and the renowned PeakFine restaurant.

The resort is the creation of founder and CEO Hans-Peter Mayr and his benefactor, the late Gernot Langes-Swarovski, patriarch of the Swarovski crystal family. Mayr was head of a wellness spa and hotel group in Austria when he fell in love with the Okanagan Valley and decided to build a European-style KurSpa here. Swarovski was delighted to invest in it.

Aside from the infinity pool, saunas and spectacular hilltop views, the highlight of a stay here is dining at PeakFine. Overseeing the restaurant is executive chef John Stratton, who's been at the resort since 2018, after living for seven years in Australia. He'd planned to hike every national park in North America, made a spontaneous decision to head west instead of east and fell in love with B.C. and the Okanagan Valley. And here he is, years later.

At PeakFine, he prides himself on serving regional food and wine, as well as a diverse menu that appeals to all guests, including those seeking a wellness experience. "I mainly use Canadian products from our B.C. seafood to our proteins and produce from the Fraser Valley area up to Salmon Arm. Everything we need is right here. Why source it from anywhere else?"

They also pride themselves on offering exceptional service. "We're in hospitality and the first thing about being in hospitality is being hospitable," Stratton says. "However, I also want to go back to the basics and highlight what we do best here in the Okanagan."

Okanagan Ribollita

At PeakFine, chef John Stratton explores a global array of flavours with dishes designed to appeal to every palate. This hearty and traditional Tuscan soup is filled with nourishing local ingredients. SERVES 6

O'Rourke's Peak
Cellars Pinot Gris

1 cup dried navy beans, soaked overnight in cold water

1 cup olive oil (divided)

3 large white onions, chopped (3 cups, divided)

6 carrots, chopped (4 cups, divided)

4 ribs celery, chopped (2 cups, divided)

7 cloves garlic, chopped (divided)

4 apples of your choice, cored and chopped (4 cups, divided)

Salt and black pepper, to taste

1 Tbsp fennel seeds

2 tsp red pepper flakes

2 tsp yellow mustard seeds

2 tsp coriander seeds

2 cups white wine (divided)

12 tomatoes, chopped

8 cups vegetable stock

6 links chicken sausage, chopped

1 leek, white and light green parts only, sliced (½ cup)

½ fennel bulb, chopped

4 sprigs thyme

¼ loaf crusty bread, torn into 1-inch pieces

½ cup chopped parsley

¼ bunch kale, chopped (1 cup)

½ cup grated Parmesan

Good-quality extra-virgin olive oil, for drizzling

Place beans in a medium saucepan and add enough cold water to cover them. Bring to a boil, then simmer for 1 hour, or until tender. Strain and set aside.

Meanwhile, heat ½ cup oil in a large stockpot over medium heat. Add 2 cups onions, 2 cups carrots, 1 cup celery, 4 cloves garlic and 2 cups apples. Season with salt and pepper. Stir for 5 minutes. Add fennel seeds, red pepper flakes, mustard seeds and coriander seeds and sauté for another 5 minutes.

Deglaze pan with 1 cup wine, then cook for 15 minutes, or until half of the liquid has been reduced. Add tomatoes and cook for another 15 minutes. Season with salt and pepper, then add stock. Bring to a boil over medium heat, then reduce heat to medium-low and gently simmer for 30 minutes.

Using a blender or immersion blender, purée soup base until smooth.

Heat the remaining ½ cup oil in a large saucepan over medium heat. Add sausage and cook for 10 to 15 minutes, until golden brown.

Add leeks, fennel, cooked navy beans and the remaining 1 cup onions, 2 cups carrots, 1 cup celery, 3 cloves garlic and 2 cups apples. Season with salt and pepper. Cook for 5 minutes. Stir in thyme and soup base and cook for 10 to 15 minutes, until vegetables are almost tender.

Stir in bread and parsley and cook for 5 minutes. Add kale and cook for 3 minutes. Season to taste with salt and black pepper.

Ladle soup into bowls and top with grated Parmesan and a drizzle of olive oil.

Truffle Mushroom Penne

Sparkling Hill Resort executive chef John Stratton loves to use the bounty of local mushrooms in this pasta dish. "It's like a mushroom alfredo with truffle and you wouldn't know it was vegan," he says. Then adds, "It's a simple weeknight meal. The cashews need to soak overnight for the cream sauce, but it can be easily made ahead of time and served as needed." SERVES 2

🍷 50th Parallel
Pinot Noir

EASY GARLIC CONFIT

3 heads garlic, separated into cloves and peeled

2 cups vegetable oil, or as needed

CREAMY CASHEW SAUCE

2 cups raw cashews

3 Tbsp nutritional yeast

2 tsp Easy Garlic Confit (about 3 to 4 cloves)

1½ tsp salt

¼ tsp white pepper

2 Tbsp white truffle oil

2 cups cold water

QUICK MUSHROOM STOCK

2 cups white mushrooms, roughly chopped

3 cups water

TRUFFLE MUSHROOM PENNE

3 Tbsp Easy Garlic Confit oil (see here)

¼ cup thinly sliced shallots

2 cloves Easy Garlic Confit (see here)

Salt and black pepper, to taste

4 cups chopped mushrooms

½ cup good white wine

1½ cups dried penne pasta

Creamy Cashew Sauce (see here)

1 cup Quick Mushroom Stock (see here)

White truffle oil, for drizzling

¼ cup chopped parsley

¼ cup chopped dill

1 Tbsp thyme leaves

Edible flowers, for garnish (optional)

EASY GARLIC CONFIT Preheat oven to 300°F.

Place garlic in a small ovenproof saucepan. Pour in enough oil to cover, then cover pan with aluminum foil. Bake for 1 to 2 hours, until garlic is deep golden brown and can be easily pierced with a knife tip. Set aside to cool.

Transfer garlic and oil to an airtight container and chill. The confit can be stored in the fridge for 2 weeks.

CREAMY CASHEW SAUCE Soak cashews in very cold water and refrigerate overnight, making sure cashews are completely submerged.

Drain cashews. In a high-power blender, combine cashews, nutritional yeast, garlic confit, salt, pepper and truffle oil and mix on low speed. Slowly increase speed to medium-high while gradually adding cold water. Blend until thick and creamy, like whipping cream. Set aside.

Creamy cashew sauce can be stored in an airtight container for up to 5 days in the fridge.

QUICK MUSHROOM STOCK Combine mushrooms and water in a saucepan. Simmer over medium heat for 45 minutes to an hour, until liquid is reduced to 1 cup.

Strain mushroom stock. Discard mushrooms or save them for soup.

TRUFFLE MUSHROOM PENNE Heat garlic oil in a large frying pan over medium-high heat until ripples appear. Add shallots and garlic confit and sauté for 5 minutes, or until shallots are translucent. Season with salt and pepper.

Add mushrooms and sauté for 10 to 15 minutes, until reduced by half. Deglaze with wine and cook for 10 to 15 minutes, until liquid has reduced by half. Season mushrooms with salt and pepper.

Meanwhile, bring a large saucepan of salted water to a boil. Add penne and cook according to package instructions. Drain.

Stir cashew sauce into the mushrooms and mix well. Stir frequently until warmed through. Add mushroom stock to create a nice, creamy texture, then add cooked penne and stir to combine. Season to taste with salt and pepper.

Divide pasta between 2 bowls. Top with a drizzle of truffle oil and the herbs. Garnish with edible flowers (if using).

SPROUT BREAD

Peter van Boekhout

KELOWNA

Peter van Boekhout calls his airy and bright bakery café "Sprout Bread," but it's a lot more than bread. It's toasts and sandwiches, coffee and pastries, salads and charcuterie. It's a hangout for young moms, keyboard warriors and nearby condo dwellers. It's a gathering place to, well, break bread.

Originally from New Zealand, van Boekhout had graduated from university and was working in coffee shops when a friend convinced him to move to Vancouver. "That's where I fell in love with baking," he says. "I was working as a barista at Nelson the Seagull a few months after they opened their doors." He later did a baking apprenticeship in Australia, then returned to Vancouver to work at Beyond Bread.

"It ticked all sorts of boxes for me, personally and professionally. I fell in love with the work," he says. He also fell in love with his wife-to-be Ava, who was from Kelowna and "floated the idea" of moving back home.

"Ever since I started working in cafés, I'd always wanted to open my own," he says. They opened in 2018 in a part of town undergoing a major makeover.

Today he makes several different kinds of bread, all from organic flour and having a thirty-six-hour fermentation. He's also expanded his menu with the addition of a talented new chef and a pastry chef.

"I feel super lucky that I get to do this every day for a living. It's romantic, but it's also hard work," van Boekhout says. "Regardless of how the day goes, at the end of the day, you've got a tangible product that is part of something that brings people together. It's very humbling."

Sprout Focaccia

Peter van Boekhout, owner and head baker at Sprout, recommends this recipe for fresh oven-baked bread before guests arrive for a dinner party. Like most bakers, he works in grams, which are more accurate than cups and tablespoons, so you will need a digital scale, as well as a digital thermometer, a bench knife, a five-quart mixer with paddle and hook attachments, and three baking pans, eight inches square and two inches deep. MAKES 3 FOCACCIA LOAVES

 Orofino Gamay

OVERNIGHT POOLISH

430 g strong, white organic bread flour

430 g warm water, at 20°C

0.5 g instant yeast

FINAL DOUGH

Overnight Poolish (see here)

300 g warm water, 40°C to 45°C

45 g olive oil, plus extra for greasing and for drizzling

2.5 g instant yeast

430 g strong, white organic bread flour, plus extra for dusting

17 g salt

OPTIONAL TOPPINGS

Rosemary leaves

Flaky sea salt, such as Maldon

Herbs and spices such as thyme, red pepper flakes or black pepper, to taste

OVERNIGHT POOLISH The night before you bake the bread, combine all ingredients in a large bowl and mix by hand until combined as a wet dough. Cover and set aside to ferment at room temperature for 12 to 16 hours, until active, bubbly and at least doubled in size.

FINAL DOUGH In a stand mixer fitted with a paddle attachment, combine poolish, water, oil and yeast. Mix on low speed for 30 seconds to break up the poolish.

Add flour and mix on the lowest speed for 3 minutes, scraping the sides of the bowl halfway through, until well mixed. Increase to medium-high speed for another 3 minutes.

Remove the paddle attachment, scraping down the attachment and edges of the bowl. Rest dough for 15 minutes.

Replace the paddle attachment with the dough hook. Add salt and mix on low speed for 3 minutes.

Transfer dough to a lightly oiled bowl. Cover bowl with a tea towel or plastic wrap and allow dough to rest at room temperature for 45 minutes.

Give the dough the first of two "folds." Wet one hand to prevent the dough from sticking, reach to the bottom of the dough, stretch it up and fold it over itself. Repeat 8 times as you spin the bowl with your free hand. Let rest, covered, for another 45 minutes. (The dough should still feel wet and slightly difficult to handle. That's okay, says van Boekhout. It should come together and gain a lot of strength by the second fold.)

Give dough a second "fold" by stretching and folding 8 more times. (Work as gently as possibly to retain the delicious gasses and delicate dough structure.) Cover and let rest for 1 hour.

Heavily flour a large work surface and oil three 8- × 8-inch baking pans.

Gently turn dough out onto the work surface and dust with flour. Using a bench knife, divide dough into three 500-g pieces and place in the prepared pans. (For a more accurate weight, you can "tare" the baking pans, or zero out their weight, on your digital scale and weigh the dough directly in the pan.) Avoid getting too much dry flour in the pans. Flip dough so the side that was face down on the work counter is now on top. If the dough does not fill the bottom of your pans, very gently press it out towards the edges with your fingertips.

Cover pans with tea towels or plastic wrap and allow to proof at room temperature for 90 minutes. Keep an eye on them and make sure the dough does not touch the cover.

Preheat oven to 500°F.

Drizzle loaves with oil. Drizzle oil over your hands and gently pat down dough, creating small dimples with your fingers. Sprinkle with rosemary, salt flakes and/or herbs and spices of your choice (if using). Let rest for 15 minutes.

Bake on the centre rack for 20 minutes, until loaves are golden brown. Transfer loaves onto a wire rack to cool.

Braised Lamb
with Burrata and Herb Oil

When Peter van Boekhout first opened Sprout, he kept things "pretty simple" in the kitchen. "It was just me and my rolling pin doing three batches of croissants a day," he says. More recently, he's hired more staff, including James McKenzie, the former restaurant chef at Waterfront Wines. "He's pushing our food in a different direction," says van Boekhout. This dish is a perfect example: it's great for a mostly make-ahead dinner, ideally served with freshly made focaccia (page 159). SERVES 6 TO 8

 Orofino Gamay

BRAISED LAMB

1½ lbs boneless lamb shoulder, cut into 2-inch cubes

3 to 4 large cloves garlic, finely chopped

1 Tbsp salt

2 tsp black pepper

2 tsp coriander seeds, ground

1½ tsp fennel seeds, ground

1 tsp smoked paprika

4 Tbsp olive oil (divided)

1 yellow onion, chopped

1 small head fennel, chopped

Pint of cherry tomatoes

1 (28-oz) can San Marzano tomatoes

1 ball fresh burrata, mozzarella or bocconcini

Sprout Focaccia (page 159), to serve

HERB OIL

5 Tbsp olive oil

1 large clove garlic, finely chopped

3 Tbsp shelled pumpkin seeds, roughly chopped

¼ cup chopped herbs, such as thyme, basil and oregano

2 pinches flaky sea salt

Pinch of crushed red pepper

2 tsp sherry vinegar or balsamic vinegar

BRAISED LAMB In a large bowl, combine lamb, garlic, salt, pepper, ground coriander, ground fennel, paprika and 1 tablespoon oil. Mix well, then refrigerate for 20 to 60 minutes.

In a separate bowl, combine onions, fennel, cherry tomatoes and 1 tablespoon oil. Toss.

Heat remaining 2 tablespoons oil in a Dutch oven over medium-high heat. Add lamb and sear on all sides, until nicely browned. Transfer lamb back to the mixing bowl.

Preheat oven to 350°F.

Add onion-tomato mixture to the Dutch oven and sauté over medium-low heat for 10 minutes, making sure no garlic or spices are stuck to the bottom. Cover and cook for 10 minutes, until tomatoes split and can be squished with the back of a spoon. Resist the urge to look or stir.

Add lamb and canned tomatoes. Cover with an ovenproof lid and braise in the oven for 2 to 2½ hours, stirring every 45 to 60 minutes, until lamb is very tender.

HERB OIL Meanwhile, heat oil in a medium saucepan over medium heat. Add garlic and pumpkin seeds and sauté for 5 minutes, just until garlic starts to brown.

Add herbs and sauté for 1 minute, until dark green and crispy-crunchy. Turn off heat and leave pan on the residual heat, until oil cools to room temperature. Just before serving, add salt, crushed red pepper and vinegar.

TO SERVE Spoon warm lamb and sauce into a large serving bowl and place burrata in the centre. Drizzle with herb oil and serve with focaccia.

TASTE OF THE OKANAGAN

Kelly Hale and Linda Murray
KELOWNA

Surrounded as they are by orchards and farms, many people in the Okanagan Valley put up preserves every summer. But in 1995, Linda Murray made it into a business that captures the very essence of the valley: Taste of the Okanagan Specialty Foods.

"My mom started the business when I was in high school, making jams and jellies out of our home kitchen. She started selling at the farmers' market, and I'd help her out on weekends," says Kelly Hale, who joined the family business in 2014. She and her husband had been working in marketing and tech overseas when Kelowna beckoned them back home.

"We were looking for a reason to move back to Canada and the opportunity to work with my mom and be close to family seemed like the best reason," Hale says. "It's a big switch from what I was doing before, but we've always been a foodie family.

I love being back in the Okanagan, surrounded by orchards and getting to work with so many amazing small farmers."

The first product out of Murray's kitchen was the red pepper jelly. "It's great on a cracker with cream cheese or on a charcuterie board and I love to cook with it," Hale says. Today, they also make chutneys, sauces, dips, dressings and seasoning mixes, all by hand in small batches, from fresh Okanagan produce, with no preservatives or additives.

Taste of the Okanagan products are available at wineries, gift shops and small specialty stores throughout B.C. Their bestseller is the bacon ketchup, but both Hale and Murray are partial to the apple chutney. "It represents the best of the Okanagan Valley," Hale says.

Although the business has grown a lot since their home kitchen, the mother-daughter team still believes you can taste the love and hard work that goes into every jar.

Autumn Bruschetta

These savoury little toasts make a perfect appetizer for both casual dinners and fancier parties. Kelly Hale tosses Taste of the Okanagan Orchard Chutney with roasted squash to make a topping that is sweet, earthy and a snap to make. SERVES 4

Haywire Switchback
Vineyard Pinot Gris

4 cups diced butternut squash

2 Tbsp olive oil (divided)

Salt and black pepper, to taste

Handful of sage leaves, thinly sliced

½ cup Taste of the Okanagan Orchard Chutney

1 baguette, cut into ½-inch slices

6 oz creamy goat cheese or ricotta

Preheat oven to 425°F. Line a baking sheet with parchment paper.

In a large bowl, combine squash, 1 tablespoon oil, salt and pepper and toss well. Spread out squash in a single layer on the prepared baking sheet. Roast for 25 minutes, tossing halfway through, until very tender.

Meanwhile, heat remaining tablespoon of oil in a frying pan over medium-high heat. Add sage and fry for 1 to 2 minutes, until crispy.

Transfer squash to a mixing bowl. Add chutney and toss.

Lightly toast baguette slices. Spread goat cheese (or ricotta) over each slice. Spoon squash mixture on top and sprinkle with fried sage.

Smoked Cheddar and Pork Burger with Grilled Okanagan Apples

Pork and apples are a match made in culinary heaven. Kelly Hale uses the apple chutney she makes for Taste of the Okanagan to add juicy flavour to these burgers—with almost no effort for you. Perfect when you just want to relax in your backyard. SERVES 4

Lunessence
Chardonnay

1½ lbs ground pork

8 oz smoked cheddar cheese, cut into ½-inch cubes

¼ cup Taste of the Okanagan Apple Chutney, plus extra for spreading

½ small white onion, finely chopped (¼ cup)

¼ cup bread crumbs

1 egg

Salt and black pepper, to taste

8 slices bacon

1 tart apple, such as Granny Smith or Pink Lady, cored and sliced into ¼-inch rings

Olive oil, for brushing

4 hamburger buns

4 tsp mayonnaise

In a large bowl, combine pork, cheese, chutney, onions, bread crumbs and egg. Mix together, but do not overwork. Season with salt and pepper. Shape into four 8-ounce patties (or 6 smaller patties), cover and refrigerate for 1 hour.

Fry bacon in a frying pan, until cooked through and crisp.

Meanwhile, preheat grill to 350°F to 400°F. Add burgers and grill for 8 to 10 minutes on each side, until fully cooked and temperature reads 160°F on an instant-read thermometer.

Brush apple slices with oil and add to the grill. Grill for 5 minutes on each side.

Transfer burgers to a plate and set aside to rest for 1 minute. Brush buns with mayonnaise and toast, mayo-side down, on the grill, until lightly brown and crisp.

Spread bottom of each bun with apple chutney, top with a patty and garnish with apple slices, bacon, and a bit more chutney. Finish with top bun and serve immediately.

TERRACE RESTAURANT AT MISSION HILL FAMILY ESTATE WINERY

Patrick Gayler
WEST KELOWNA

When it comes to wine-country dining, Mission Hill is the OG. It was one of B.C.'s premier estate wineries, opened by Anthony von Mandl in 1981; the first to win an international wine award; and its Terrace Restaurant was one of B.C.'s first winery restaurants. Six years after it first opened in 2002, *Travel + Leisure* named it one of the world's top five winery restaurants.

Keeping it at the top is executive chef Patrick Gayler. Originally from Edmonton, he worked at Calgary's Catch and Victoria's Inn at Laurel Point and was a member of Culinary Team Canada for three years before joining Mission Hill in 2014.

"It's been challenging and incredibly rewarding," he says. "Sourcing the best seasonal Okanagan ingredients, getting them into the kitchens and then onto our menus requires constant focus and planning. Executive sous chef Adam Vaughan and chef de cuisine Heather Brumwell really take it to heart and do a phenomenal job of showcasing our valley."

He adds: "Without a doubt, our team's greatest success has been building such close relationships with our farmers and winemakers. Their insight and support have been integral to the winery's success."

That's allowed them to make more products in house, including the honey harvested from their own hives and the charcuterie made from nearby sustainably raised pork, and to hone their wine and food pairings.

Most of all, he likes to keep things simple, allowing the ingredients and the wine to speak for themselves. "When you can get fresh and seasonal local ingredients, you don't have to do much to them," Gayler says. "We're super fortunate."

Okanagan Spring Asparagus, Morel and Sunchoke Soup

At Mission Hill, spring means asparagus and asparagus means Sauvignon Blanc. "A number of natural wine pairings come up in spring," says executive chef Patrick Gayler. Mission Hill was the valley's first winery restaurant to focus on local ingredients and, indeed, to grow its own. Here, chef Gayler sources asparagus from local farmers, morel mushrooms from local foragers and fresh herbs from his own garden. SERVES 4

🍷 **Mission Hill Reserve Sauvignon Blanc**

2 lbs asparagus, stems sliced into thin discs, tips reserved for garnish and woody bottoms used for stock

2 cups water

6 Tbsp butter

1 leek, white and light green parts only, thinly sliced

1½ cups loosely packed basil leaves, plus extra for garnish

½ cup loosely packed cilantro leaves, plus extra for garnish

½ cup loosely packed tarragon leaves, plus extra for garnish

1 lb sunchokes, peeled and roughly chopped

2 cups milk, plus extra if needed

Salt and black pepper, to taste

¼ cup good-quality olive oil

½ clove garlic, finely chopped

1 cup sliced morel mushrooms

½ cup yogurt, for garnish

In a medium saucepan, combine woody asparagus stems and water. Bring to a boil, then reduce heat and simmer for 15 minutes. Strain and reserve stock.

Melt butter in the same saucepan over medium heat. Add leeks and herbs and sauté for 2 minutes, until tender and aromatic. Add sunchokes, 1 cup asparagus stock and the milk. Simmer for 20 minutes, until sunchokes are tender and falling apart.

Transfer to a blender and blend until smooth. Return mixture to a clean saucepan. If needed, add more milk or stock to achieve desired consistency. Season with salt and pepper. Bring to a gentle simmer. Add in the sliced asparagus stalks and gently simmer for 2 to 3 minutes.

Meanwhile, heat oil in a medium frying pan over medium-high heat. Add garlic, asparagus tips and morels and sauté for 1 to 2 minutes. Remove from heat. Season well with salt and pepper.

Arrange asparagus tips and mushrooms in 4 soup bowls. If you like, drizzle residual olive oil from the pan into the bowls.

Transfer soup to the blender again and blend until smooth. Ladle soup into the bowls. Finish with a dollop of yogurt and more herbs.

Roasted B.C. Halibut with Dill, New Potatoes and Corn-Glazed Cauliflower

Freshly caught halibut is one of the treasures of the west coast of B.C.: tender yet firm, mild but rich—and delightful when seared to a caramelized crust. Here, Mission Hill's executive chef Patrick Gayler serves it with humble vegetables and a fragrant dill "pistou," which is similar to pesto but made without nuts or cheese. SERVES 4

🍷 Mission Hill Perpetua Chardonnay

HALIBUT

4 (4-oz) skinless halibut portions

POTATOES

1 lb new potatoes, such as Sieglinde or fingerling
1 shallot, sliced
1 clove garlic, crushed
1 cup apple juice
Grated zest and juice of 1 lemon
Pinch of salt
Pinch of black pepper

DILL PISTOU

4 oz dill, leaves chopped and stems reserved (about 2 cups)
½ clove garlic, finely chopped
¼ cup olive oil
2 Tbsp water
2 tsp grainy mustard
Grated zest of 1 lemon
Salt and black pepper, to taste

ASSEMBLY

2 Tbsp butter (divided)
1 cup cauliflower florets
¼ cup reserved potato cooking liquid (see here), plus extra if needed
4 ears of corn, shucked
Salt and black pepper, to taste
2 Tbsp canola or grapeseed oil
6 to 10 reserved dill stems (see here)
1 lemon, quartered and seeded
2 lemons, halved and grilled, for garnish (optional)

HALIBUT Place halibut portions in the fridge on a paper towel–lined plate for 2 to 3 hours to dry out. This helps prevent the fish from sticking to the pan so it can brown properly.

POTATOES In a medium saucepan, combine potatoes, shallots, garlic, apple juice and lemon juice and zest. Add salt and pepper and enough water to just cover potatoes. Bring to a simmer, then cover with a tight-fitting lid and cook for 15 minutes, until potatoes are fork tender. Remove from the heat and set aside to cool to room temperature.

Strain cooking liquid into a bowl and reserve for later. Halve or quarter potatoes to desired size.

DILL PISTOU Using a mortar and pestle or food processor, grind all ingredients except the dill stems together until it has a pesto-like consistency. Season with salt and pepper. Set aside.

ASSEMBLY Melt 1 tablespoon butter in a frying pan over medium-high heat. Add cauliflower and sauté for 5 minutes, until lightly golden brown. Add potatoes and ¼ cup potato cooking liquid and warm through. Stir in corn and sauté for 3 minutes. If needed, add more potato cooking liquid to create a saucy, chowder-like consistency. Season to taste with salt and pepper. Keep warm.

Heat oil in a large heavy-bottomed frying pan until just beginning to smoke. Season halibut generously with salt and pat the surface dry with a paper towel. Once pan is hot, carefully press fish into it. Sear for 1 to 2 minutes, then flip over and sear for another 3 to 4 minutes, until edges brown and halibut is golden. If oil begins to smoke heavily, remove the pan from the heat for 1 minute to cool slightly.

Turn off the heat and flip halibut over. Add dill stems and the remaining 1 tablespoon butter and baste for 30 seconds until fragrant and fish is slightly caramelized. Squeeze lemon quarters overtop. Be sure not to overcook the halibut. It should have some firmness to it and just flake slightly to your touch. If slightly uncooked, rest in the warm frying pan for another minute.

Distribute the potato and cauliflower mixture evenly among 4 bowls. Top with halibut and dill pistou, and garnish with grilled lemon halves (if using).

THE TERRACE RESTAURANT
AT MONTE CREEK WINERY

Romeo Oloresisimo
KAMLOOPS

Hot days, cool nights and limestone-rich soil give a bright, crisp, minerally freshness to the wines grown along the South Thompson River. "The fresh acidity in the South Thompson is what makes wine so food-friendly," says Ashley Demedeiros, the marketing manager at Monte Creek Winery.

When the winery first opened in June 2015, it offered meat and cheese boards for guests to enjoy. "It was our first season, and we wanted to take things slow. The support was overwhelming, and guests wanted a more full-service restaurant experience," Demedeiros says.

And now they have one.

They reached out to Romeo Oloresisimo, the executive chef of Romeo's Kitchen + Spirits in the Coast Kamloops Hotel downtown, to provide the food for the seasonal outdoor terrace. He'd relocated from Vancouver to Kamloops, his wife's hometown, in 2011. "I call this home," he says. "It's a growing city for sure. It's quiet, simple and affordable. We do have a young family, so that's important to us."

The classically trained chef had grown up eating food from Vancouver's myriad cultures, and his menu is just as globetrotting, including Mexico-inspired tacos, Middle Eastern snacks, Italian pizzas and paninis, Jamaican patties and Asian Buddha bowls. "Food is food. I don't set boundaries with what I do," he says.

This partnership has proved highly popular among both locals and visitors. "The Terrace menu has an eclectic global feel but sourced locally," says Demedeiros.

Moroccan Dip

Chef Romeo Oloresisimo brings a globetrotting palate to his menu for Monte Creek, and among the most popular dishes he serves is this Moroccan-inspired dip. Not quite a traditional hummus, it is fragrant with ras el hanout, a Middle Eastern spice blend traditionally used for chicken, lamb, grilled veggies, eggs and couscous. A perfect patio snack, it is also delicious with the kind of aromatic white wines Monte Creek is known for. SERVES 2 TO 4

Monte Creek Living Land Riesling

RAS EL HANOUT

1 tsp ground cinnamon

1 tsp paprika

1 tsp ground cumin

1 tsp ground coriander

¼ tsp cayenne pepper

¼ tsp ground allspice

MOROCCAN DIP

1½ Tbsp vegetable oil

½ white onion, chopped

2 cloves garlic, finely chopped

1 (1-inch) piece ginger, peeled and finely chopped

2 tsp Ras El Hanout (see here)

1 tsp salt

2 Roma tomatoes, chopped

1 cup canned chickpeas with their liquid

¼ cup chopped cilantro

2 cups vegetable stock

TO SERVE

3 to 4 oz fresh goat cheese

1 tsp Ras El Hanout (see here), for sprinkling

Mango chutney

Flatbread, such as pita or naan, warmed

RAS EL HANOUT Combine all ingredients in a jar. Close lid and shake well.

MOROCCAN DIP Heat oil in a large frying pan over medium heat. Add onions and sauté for 5 to 7 minutes, until soft and translucent. Reduce heat to medium-low. Stir in garlic, ginger, ras el hanout and salt and cook for another 3 minutes.

Add remaining ingredients. Reduce heat to low and simmer for 1 hour. Transfer to a bowl and let cool to room temperature. Chill in the fridge for at least 24 hours.

If you prefer a smoother dip, you can purée it in a food processor before serving.

TO SERVE Reheat the dip in a frying pan over medium-low heat. Transfer to a heatproof serving bowl (chef suggests a tagine). Crumble goat cheese on top, then sprinkle with ras el hanout and garnish with a spoonful of mango chutney.

Serve with warm flatbreads.

Beef Barbacoa

When chef Romeo Oloresisimo was asked to prepare the food for Monte Creek winery, he created a menu of easygoing, globally inspired dishes like this Mexican-flavoured braised beef dish. It's best served in a taco or burrito, along with the pepita sauce and whatever other toppings you like. And, of course, a generous glass of Monte Creek's limestone-enhanced wines. SERVES 4

Monte Creek Living Land Cabernet Franc

BARBACOA PASTE

3 ancho chilies
6 pasilla chilies
2 tomatoes
2 tsp black peppercorns
2 tsp cumin seeds
3 cloves garlic
1 yellow onion, roughly chopped
2 tsp dried oregano
1 tsp ground cinnamon
½ cup apple cider vinegar
55 g (½ package) achiote paste (see Note)

BRAISED BEEF

2 lbs boneless beef short ribs or other stewing beef, diced into 1-inch cubes
Barbacoa Paste (see here)
1 to 2 Tbsp vegetable oil
5 cloves garlic, chopped
1 large white onion, chopped
8 tomatillos, chopped
3 Roma tomatoes, chopped
2 stalks celery, chopped
4 cups chicken stock
2 cups root beer
Small corn or flour tortillas, to serve
Chopped white onions, chopped cilantro and/ or lime wedges, to serve (optional)

PEPITA SAUCE

1 tomatillo
3 cloves garlic
1 to 2 jalapeño peppers, stemmed and seeded
1¾ cups shelled pumpkin seeds (pepitas)
Bunch of cilantro, leaves only
⅔ cup vegetable oil
Juice of 1 lime
Salt and black pepper, to taste

BARBACOA PASTE Preheat oven to 350°F.

Place chilies on a baking sheet and toast for 10 minutes. Set aside to cool, then remove stem and seeds.

Place chilies in a heatproof bowl of boiling water. Soak for 20 minutes. Transfer chilies to a food processor (or blender). Reserve soaking water.

Meanwhile, preheat a grill or broiler to high heat. Blister tomatoes on all sides. Add to food processor.

Toast peppercorns and cumin seeds in a small frying pan over medium heat for 2 to 3 minutes. Set aside to cool slightly. Transfer spices to a spice grinder or mortar and pestle and grind. Add to food processor, along with garlic, onions, oregano, cinnamon, vinegar and achiote. Blend until a smooth paste forms. If paste is too thick to blend easily, add a little reserved chili water to thin it out.

BRAISED BEEF In a large non-reactive bowl, mix beef and barbacoa paste. Refrigerate and allow to marinate for 4 hours.

Preheat oven to 300°F.

Heat oil in a Dutch oven over medium heat. Add garlic and onions and sauté for 5 minutes, until softened and translucent. Add tomatillos, tomatoes and celery and sauté for 10 minutes, until soft and fragrant. Stir in marinated meat, then pour in stock and root beer. Mix well.

Cover with an ovenproof lid and braise for 3 to 4 hours, stirring occasionally, until tender.

PEPITA SAUCE Meanwhile, bring a small saucepan of water to a boil. Add the tomatillo and blanch for 5 minutes, until soft. Transfer to a bowl of cold water to cool. Roughly chop tomatillo and transfer to a blender or food processor. Add remaining ingredients and blend until smooth. Set aside in a small bowl and cover until needed.

TO SERVE Warm tortillas in the oven, then heap braised beef on the tortillas and top with pepita sauce. If you like, you can add other toppings such as chopped onions, cilantro and/or a squeeze of lime.

NOTE Achiote is a spice and colouring agent commonly used in Mexican and Caribbean dishes. It is extracted from the seeds of an evergreen shrub and can be used whole or ground, as a paste or oil. It has a mild peppery flavour and is often used interchangeably with annatto. You can find achiote at specialty markets or order it online.

TERRAFINA RESTAURANT AT HESTER CREEK

Adair Scott
OLIVER

In 1968, a pioneer named Joe Busnardo planted what were likely the first *Vitis vinifera*, the noble grapes that produce the world's great wines, in the Okanagan Valley. He brought vine clippings from his native Italy and planted them on the grounds of what is now Hester Creek Estate Winery. Fifty-plus years later, some of those vines are still producing great wine.

That's quite the legacy for restaurant chef Adair Scott to work with.

"To walk into the cellar and find the winemaker pulling wine out of a barrel, is just inspiring and puts me in a good headspace," he says. "It's great that we have such a large portfolio."

Scott joined Terrafina in February 2020, after seven years cooking at Watermark Beach Resort in Osoyoos (page 18). Originally from Prince George, he also created "beach luxe" cuisine in Australia and at a golf course in Kelowna.

The Mediterranean-themed Terrafina (the name means "fine earth") is nestled among the vines on the property. Here, Scott assembles the restaurant's epic antipasti boards, famous truffle potato pizza

and other dishes that pair easily with Hester Creek's extensive portfolio. In the tasting room nearby, he also leads cooking classes in the opulent demo kitchen.

"I'm trying to keep the food and wine local and sustainable," he says. "We planted a massive garden out back with peach, nectarine and plum trees. We put beehives on the roof of the winery so I can use our own honey." He also forages. "If I didn't go out in the forest, I would go out of my mind."

He adds, "Hester Creek does such a great job in supporting local agriculture as well as making wine."

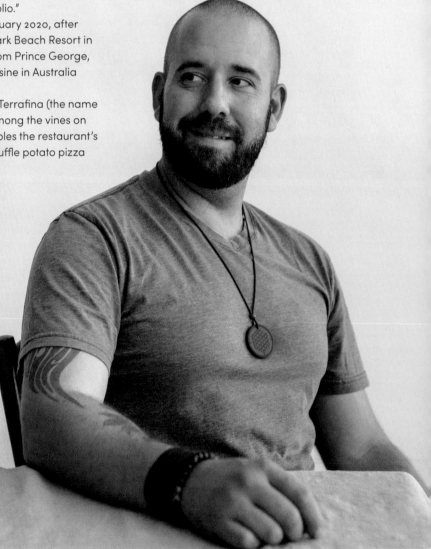

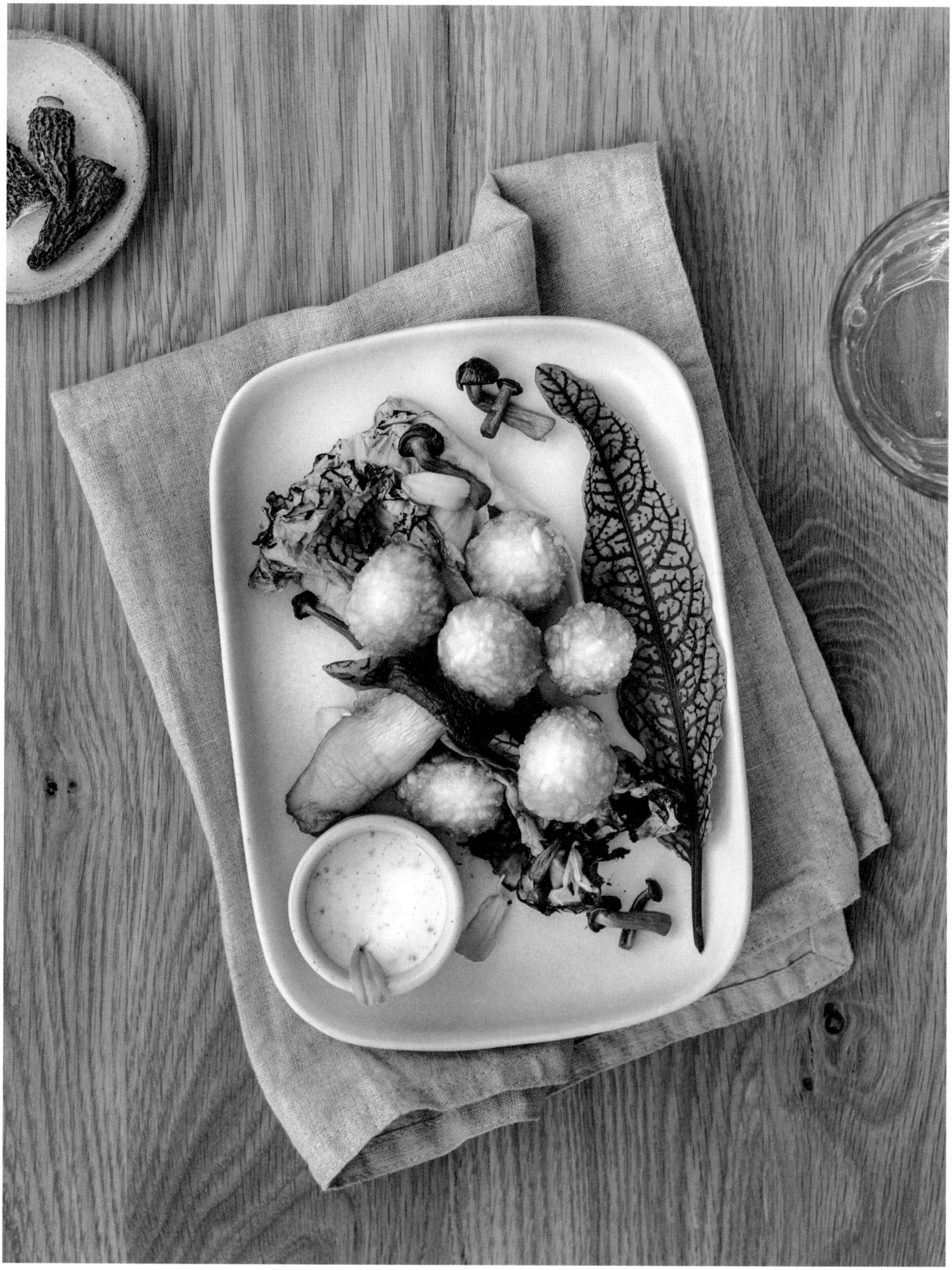

Wild Mushroom Arancini, p. 178

Wild Mushroom Arancini

Terrafina chef Adair Scott likes to forage in the hills and forests around the South Okanagan, where he can find a variety of wild mushrooms, and especially the morels that are so abundant after a fire. You may need to forage at the grocery store instead—look for a mix of mushrooms that can include morels, chanterelles, oysters and cremini. SERVES 4

Hester Creek Estate Winery Source Collection Chardonnay

RICE AND MUSHROOMS
1 Tbsp olive oil or butter
1 cup chopped wild mushrooms
3 cups chicken stock
1 cup arborio rice

TRUFFLE AIOLI
2 eggs
1 Tbsp white vinegar
1 Tbsp Dijon mustard
1 tsp lemon juice
½ tsp black pepper
½ tsp salt
¾ cup canola oil
1 Tbsp truffle oil

ASSEMBLY
Rice and Mushrooms (see here)
½ cup grated Parmesan
2 Tbsp chopped Italian parsley
Salt and black pepper, to taste
2 eggs, beaten
1½ cups fine bread crumbs
Canola oil, for frying
Charred greens, sautéed mushrooms and edible flowers, for garnish (optional)

RICE AND MUSHROOMS Heat oil (or butter) in a frying pan over medium heat. Add mushrooms and sauté for 10 to 15 minutes, until soft. Set aside.

Bring stock to a boil in a saucepan over medium-high heat. Stir in rice, then reduce heat to low and simmer uncovered for 20 minutes, until tender and liquid is absorbed.

Line a baking sheet with parchment paper. Spread cooked rice on the baking sheet and set aside to cool completely.

TRUFFLE AIOLI Meanwhile, combine all ingredients, except oils, in a food processor and blend until smooth. With the motor still running, gradually add oils and blend until emulsified and a mayonnaise texture results. (If the oil is added too fast, the sauce will split and you will need to start over.) Chill aioli until ready to serve.

ASSEMBLY In a bowl, combine cooled rice, sautéed mushrooms, Parmesan, parsley and salt and pepper to taste. Stir in eggs. Spread bread crumbs out in a shallow bowl.

Using your hands, roll rice mixture into balls, each about 2 inches in diameter. You should have 8 to 12 balls.

Heat a couple inches of oil in a small, deep saucepan until the temperature reaches 350°F. Roll rice balls in bread crumbs and gently lower into pan, working in batches if necessary to prevent overcrowding. Fry for 3 minutes, until golden and crispy on all sides. Transfer to a paper towel–lined plate to drain.

Serve arancini warm topped with truffle aioli. If you like, serve charred greens and sautéed mushrooms beside the arancini, and garnish with edible flowers.

Rosemary Lamb Chops with Gnocchi

Some of Hester Creek Estate Winery's most famous wines are its big, bold, fruit-forward red blends, especially The Judge, a Bordeaux-style blend of Merlot, Cabernet Sauvignon and Cabernet Franc from some of the oldest vines in the Okanagan Valley. This simple but luxurious dish from chef Adair Scott makes a perfect partner for it. SERVES 4

Hester Creek Estate Winery The Judge Red Blend

POTATO GNOCCHI

4 large russet potatoes, unpeeled

½ cup flour, plus extra for dusting

½ cup grated Parmesan

¼ tsp ground nutmeg

Pinch of salt and black pepper

1 Tbsp vegetable oil, plus extra for greasing

1 Tbsp butter

LAMB CHOPS

2 racks of lamb, frenched

3 Tbsp chopped rosemary

1 Tbsp coarse salt

1 tsp black pepper

1 Tbsp vegetable oil

POTATO GNOCCHI Place potatoes in a saucepan of cold water and bring to a boil. Boil for 15 to 20 minutes, until fully cooked and skin begins to split. Drain, then transfer to a baking sheet and refrigerate until cooled. (Better yet, refrigerate them overnight to dry out potatoes entirely.)

Peel potatoes, then transfer to a bowl and mash until smooth. (Alternatively, put them through a ricer or food mill.) You should have 350 g (1¼ cups) of potatoes. Add flour, Parmesan, nutmeg, salt and pepper and mix well.

Transfer dough to a clean work surface and knead for 5 to 10 minutes, until it becomes a smooth ball. Dust with flour as needed. Divide dough into four equal portions. Working with one piece of dough, roll into an even rope, about 1 inch in diameter. Cut into 1-inch pieces and place on a floured baking sheet. Repeat with the remaining dough.

Bring a large saucepan of salted water to a boil. Working in batches to avoid overcrowding, gently lower gnocchi into the pan and blanch for 10 seconds, until gnocchi float to the surface. Using a slotted spoon, transfer gnocchi to a lightly oiled baking sheet. Set aside to cool to room temperature.

Heat butter and oil in a large frying pan over medium heat. Add gnocchi and pan-fry for 3 to 5 minutes until golden. Keep warm.

LAMB CHOPS Cut lamb racks between the bones into individual chops. In a small bowl, combine rosemary, salt and pepper. Drizzle lamb chops with oil and rub with spice blend.

Preheat a grill or cast-iron frying pan over medium-high heat. Add chops and grill (or pan-fry) for 2 minutes on each side, until desired doneness is achieved. Set aside to rest for 2 to 3 minutes. Transfer to a serving plate and serve warm with potato gnocchi.

TIMBER SHUSWAP

Chris Whittaker

BLIND BAY

"The reason we came up here was because I knew what it was like to be raised in a small community," says chef Chris Whittaker. "Hunting, fishing, gathering, they were all at the forefront of what I wanted to do. I was at a point where I wanted to reconnect with all that."

"Up here" is Blind Bay, near Shuswap Lake, northeast of the Okanagan Valley. Visitors come to the Shuswap for the houseboating or to check out the epic salmon spawning runs on the Adams River. But if Whittaker has his way, they'll soon be coming for the food.

Originally from Thunder Bay, he had been cooking in Vancouver's Listel Hotel for several years when he, his wife Marianne and their young son felt the countryside calling to them. After a couple years at the Indigenous-owned Quaaout Lodge, he partnered with friends Lisa and Sean McLean, who own a beef ranch, to open his own restaurant, Timber Shuswap.

This charmingly rustic space is the rebirth of Timber Vancouver, the Canadiana-themed gastropub he introduced back at the Listel.

Here, he's serving classically inspired, ingredient-driven dishes with a touch of international influence. "I'm calling it Canadian cuisine because that's what it is," he says.

"The Shuswap is coming into its own," he adds. "The restaurants are in the infancy of what they can be. We have awesome dairy producers, egg producers, even rabbit producers, and they are all willing to work with you."

A proud Shuswapian, he is passionate about being a steward for the land, and says, "I'm just up here trying to represent the Shuswap the best way we can, using local ingredients and local farms."

Steak with French Beans, Heirloom Tomatoes, Toasted Hazelnuts and Fresh Herbs

As chef Chris Whittaker's partners own a cattle ranch, beef naturally plays an important role on his menu. But it also speaks to the heritage of the region, which has long been cattle country. Here, he uses flank steak, a lean, flavourful and versatile cut that is less expensive than most prime cuts, and popular with chefs. If you cannot find it at the supermarket, ask your butcher. SERVES 3 TO 4

Covert Farms Grand Reserve Cabernet Sauvignon

STEAK

1 (1-lb) flank steak, cleaned and trimmed

1 clove garlic, finely chopped

¼ tsp ground cinnamon

Salt and black pepper, to taste

¼ cup red miso paste or liquid from fermented tofu

3 Tbsp sesame oil

2 Tbsp maple syrup

1 tsp Sriracha

VEGETABLES

1 lb green beans, thinly sliced diagonally

1 Tbsp vegetable oil

½ lb heirloom tomatoes or cherry tomatoes

6 Tbsp olive oil

2 Tbsp wildflower honey

1 Tbsp seasoned rice vinegar

1 Tbsp Dijon mustard

Grated zest and juice of 1 orange

GARNISHES

1 cup toasted and chopped hazelnuts

8 oz mixed herbs, such as Italian parsley, purslane, chives and wild chamomile

STEAK The night before, combine all ingredients in a zip-top bag and mix well. Allow to marinate overnight in the fridge.

The next day, preheat a grill over high heat. Pat steak dry, then grill for 2 to 3 minutes on each side for rare to medium-rare. Let rest for 10 minutes.

VEGETABLES Bring a saucepan of salted water to a boil. Prepare an ice bath. Add beans to the pan and blanch for 10 seconds. Using a slotted spoon, transfer beans to the ice bath. Remove from ice bath and pat beans dry with a clean towel.

Heat vegetable oil in a large frying pan over high heat. Add beans and tomatoes and sauté for about 10 minutes, until tomatoes blister. Remove from heat.

In a medium bowl, whisk together olive oil, honey, vinegar, mustard and orange zest and juice. Add beans and tomatoes and toss gently.

Thinly slice steak and arrange on a platter. Add warm tomatoes and beans, then drizzle pan juices over the veg. Garnish with hazelnuts and fresh herbs.

Soft Farm Egg, Morel Mushroom Soy, Crispy Bits and Chives

At Timber Shuswap, chef Chris Whittaker serves these poached eggs as a light, savoury snack. The mushrooms and soy add a complex layer of umami while the fried potato adds an appealing crunch to contrast with the soft egg. Consider this the new deconstructed, vegetarian, gourmet version of that old pub favourite, the Scotch egg. SERVES 4

Meyer Family
Vineyards Micro
Cuvée Chardonnay

4 cups water (divided)

¼ cup white vinegar, plus extra if needed

1 small Kennebec potato, peeled and thinly sliced

8 to 10 dried morel mushrooms

¼ cup high-quality soy sauce

1 Tbsp sambal oelek (Indonesian chili paste)

3 cups vegetable oil (divided)

8 cloves garlic, thinly sliced

4 free-range eggs

¼ cup finely chopped chives

Chive blossoms, for garnish (optional)

Bring 3 cups of water to a boil in a saucepan. Add vinegar, then reduce heat to medium and add potato slices. Cook for 3 minutes, or until just tender. Drain, then transfer to a tray and dry in the fridge for 2 hours or up to overnight.

Bring the remaining 1 cup water to a boil in a small saucepan. Place mushrooms in a heatproof bowl, then pour the boiling water over them. Set aside for 30 minutes until mushrooms are softened.

Strain mushroom soaking liquid into a small saucepan and simmer over medium heat until reduced to 2 tablespoons. Finely slice morels, then add them to the pan. Stir in soy sauce and sambal oelek. Set aside.

Combine 1 cup of oil and the sliced garlic in a small saucepan. Slowly warm over medium heat for 10 to 15 minutes, until garlic turns golden brown and crispy. Transfer to a paper towel–lined plate to drain.

Heat remaining 2 cups oil in a deep saucepan to a temperature of 300°F. Add dried potato slices and fry for 5 minutes, until golden. Transfer to a paper towel–lined plate to drain.

Chop crispy potatoes and garlic until fine. Transfer to a bowl and mix well.

Set a circulator (or sous-vide unit) to 150°F. Place eggs in the circulator and cook for 45 minutes until soft poached. (Alternatively, you can soft poach eggs in 4 cups of simmering water with a tablespoon of white vinegar for 3 minutes.)

Divide eggs among four bowls and top each with 1 teaspoon of morel soy, 1 tablespoon potato-garlic crumb and a sprinkling of chives. Garnish with chive blossoms (if using).

VINEYARD KITCHEN AND PATIO AT NIGHTHAWK VINEYARDS

Carson Bibby
OKANAGAN FALLS

Head to the hills—way up into the hills—near Okanagan Falls to discover one of B.C.'s highest-altitude wineries and the exciting, locally inspired food produced by its chef. That chef is Carson Bibby, whose parents Daniel and Christy own the winery, and whose brother Dakota is the winemaker.

"My parents were big wine fans for a long time. We were living in Kelowna and my family decided they didn't want to leave the Okanagan," Carson says. "I came home from school and they were so excited: We found a deal!"

Carson had been studying at Okanagan College, cooking at Liquidity Wines and assisting competing chefs at the Canadian Culinary Championships in Kelowna. Gold medalist Marc Lepine was so impressed, he hired Carson as chef de partie for his Ottawa restaurant Atelier. A year later, Carson staged at London's Savoy Hotel, then became chef at Bella Italia in Sun Peaks, before returning to Okanagan Falls.

"We are an outdoor patio restaurant," says Carson. "We're primarily focused on our wood-burning forno oven from Portugal. Everything on the menu ends up hitting the oven in some way. The cherrywood gives a nice smoky flavour."

Mostly that means pizza, but they also serve salads, sandwiches, charcuterie boards and a popular cast-iron baked brie, all of which go nicely with Nighthawk's bright, flavourful wines.

The dining may be casual, but they still use Riedel crystal and quality linens. "It's elegant casual dining," Carson says. "Cooking outside is a very different experience. You have to deal with the wind, and we even had to close for a couple days during the heat wave."

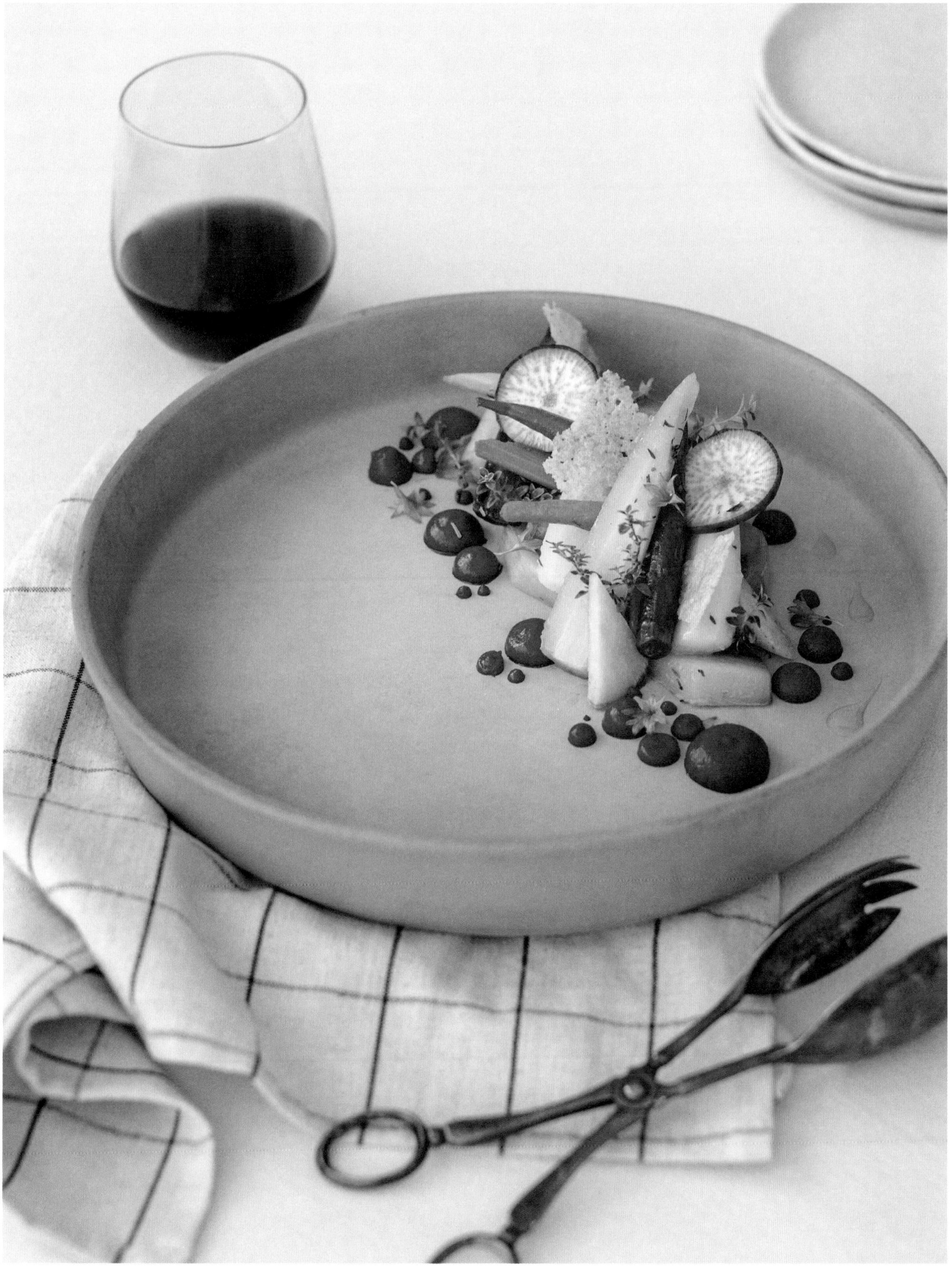

Family Roots Salad, p. 186

Family Roots Salad

Nighthawk Vineyards is truly a family business, owned by Daniel and Christy Bibby, with sons Dakota making the wine and Carson manning the kitchen. Here, Carson celebrates those family roots while also dishing up layers of sweet, earthy root vegetables. SERVES 4

🍷 Nighthawk Vineyards
Pinot Noir

PICKLED PARSNIPS
8 black peppercorns
3 sprigs thyme
2 sprigs tarragon
1 bay leaf
2 Tbsp sugar
1 tsp fennel seeds
1 tsp salt
½ tsp dried savory
¾ cup white vinegar
1¼ cups water
3 parsnips, peeled and cut into ½-inch batons

BEET PURÉE
1½ medium beets, peeled and quartered
1 Tbsp butter
1 tsp lemon juice
1 tsp salt

ROOT VEGETABLES
2 medium golden beets
2 Tbsp honey (divided)
Lemon-infused olive oil or other high-quality olive oil, such as Coppini Arte Olearia Olive and Lemon Condimento
Lemon-thyme or traditional fleur de sel
4 yellow heirloom carrots, unpeeled and scrubbed clean
4 orange heirloom carrots, unpeeled and scrubbed clean
4 purple heirloom carrots, unpeeled and scrubbed clean
½ cup grated Parmesan

ASSEMBLY
2 purple radishes, thinly sliced
Edible flowers, for garnish

PICKLED PARSNIPS Place all ingredients, except parsnips, in a large heavy-bottomed saucepan and bring to a boil. Reduce heat to medium-low, add parsnips and simmer for 5 minutes. Remove from heat and cool. Transfer parsnips and liquid to a 1-litre Mason jar. This quick pickle can be stored for up to 3 weeks in the fridge.

BEET PURÉE Place beets in a saucepan of water over medium-high heat and boil for 20 minutes, until tender. Drain, then transfer to a blender or food processor. Add butter, lemon juice and salt and purée until smooth. Pass purée through fine-mesh sieve and set aside to cool. Pour mixture into a squeeze bottle.

ROOT VEGETABLES Place golden beets in a saucepan of water and boil for 20 minutes, until tender. Drain, then cut into 6 wedges each. Place in a small bowl and coat with a tablespoon of honey and a little lemon olive oil. Sprinkle with fleur de sel and set aside.

Preheat broiler.

Bring a saucepan of water to a boil. Add carrots and blanch for 30 seconds. Drain, then cut in half lengthwise. Transfer to a bowl and toss with the remaining 1 tablespoon honey and a little lemon olive oil. Transfer to a baking sheet and broil for 10 minutes, until they start to brown. Remove from oven and set aside to cool.

Preheat oven to 400°F. Line a baking sheet with parchment paper.

Using a tablespoon, scoop piles of Parmesan onto the prepared baking sheet and lightly pat down. Makes about 8 mounds. Bake for 3 to 5 minutes, until golden brown and crisp. Set aside to cool.

ASSEMBLY Arrange golden beets, carrots and pickled parsnips together on individual plates. Using a squeeze bottle, dot drops of beet purée around each plate. Garnish with radishes, edible flowers and Parmesan crisps. Finish with a drizzle of lemon oil and a sprinkling of fleur de sel.

Okanagan Delight

Like a granola bar, only topped with a peach syrup and a decadent raspberry-flavoured white chocolate ganache, Carson Bibby's beautifully layered dessert bar captures all the flavours and textures of the Okanagan Valley. MAKES 18 BARS

 Nighthawk Vineyards Merlot

CRUNCHY BASE

1½ cups toasted rolled oats

3 Tbsp toasted sunflower seeds

½ cup finely chopped dried apricots

½ cup chopped soft apple chips

¼ cup dark maple syrup

3 Tbsp honey

2 Tbsp butter

½ cup lightly packed brown sugar

½ tsp ground sumac

JAMMY CENTRE

1 cup sugar

⅔ cup + ½ cup water (divided)

½ tsp citric acid

3 Tbsp cornstarch

⅔ cup peach juice

GANACHE TOPPING

6 oz chopped white chocolate (preferably Callebaut)

3½ Tbsp whipping (33%) cream

1 Tbsp raspberry fortified wine (preferably Elephant Island Orchard Framboise)

7 drops red food colouring

CRUNCHY BASE Line a deep 9-inch-square baking dish with parchment paper.

In a stainless steel bowl, combine oats, sunflower seeds, apricots and apple chips. Set aside.

Combine maple syrup, honey, butter, brown sugar and sumac in a small, heavy-bottomed saucepan. Heat over medium heat to a temperature of 245°F (soft-ball stage).

Working quickly, stir liquid mixture into dry ingredients. Transfer to the prepared baking dish, then press evenly into the dish while still hot. Set aside to fully cool.

JAMMY CENTRE Meanwhile, combine sugar, ⅔ cup water and citric acid in a small heavy-bottomed saucepan. Heat over medium heat until the temperature reaches 250°F (hard-ball stage).

In a bowl, combine cornstarch, peach juice and ½ cup water. Mix until smooth.

Carefully whisk in cornstarch mixture over medium heat until syrup starts to thicken. (If you work too quickly, it will boil over.) Reduce heat to low and gently simmer for 45 minutes, until thick and syrupy. Pour over the cooled oat mixture and set aside for at least 4 hours.

GANACHE TOPPING Place chocolate in a microwave-safe bowl. Partially melt chocolate by microwaving it in 15-second intervals, stirring it after each interval. (Do not overheat, to avoid splitting.) Set aside.

Heat cream in a saucepan to just under a boil. Pour cream over chocolate and fold in wine and food colouring. Mix well. Pour ganache evenly over the set layers of the dessert. Refrigerate overnight.

Slice into 1-inch squares and serve.

WAYNE & FREDA

Jen and Ryan Hawk
PENTICTON

Wayne & Freda is a homecoming for Jen and Ryan Hawk. "I grew up in Summerland, and Ryan spent his summers here," Jen recalls. "We both had these idyllic childhoods."

Just a few years ago, they were still living in Vancouver, where she was an interior designer for high-rise developments and he co-owned an indoor golf bar. They'd met over a crib game and discovered that they both had a grandparent living in the same care facility in Summerland. When Ryan's grandfather Wayne and Jen's grandmother Freda learned their grandkids were dating each other, the staff arranged for them to sit together during meals.

"They had this really sweet friendship," Jen says. "We loved it and we wanted to honour them."

In 2017, after fifteen years in Vancouver, the Hawks were missing home. "Our son was turning one, and we liked the idea of being closer to family and a slower lifestyle," Jen says. They sold their house, came back to the valley without a plan, and travelled across Asia for three months. As they travelled, they realized that they wanted to work together and eventually decided to open a great coffee shop in Penticton. "There seemed to be a gap in the market," Jen says.

They found an old upholstery shop/garage where Jen could put her interior design expertise to work, and Ryan his handyman skills. They now have a hundred-seat café where they serve smoothies, baked goods, bowls, granolas, toasts, sandwiches and, of course, excellent coffee. And, in the spirit of its namesakes, Wayne & Freda has become a gathering place for the community.

"We just fell in love with the Okanagan," Jen says. "It's one of the most beautiful places on Earth."

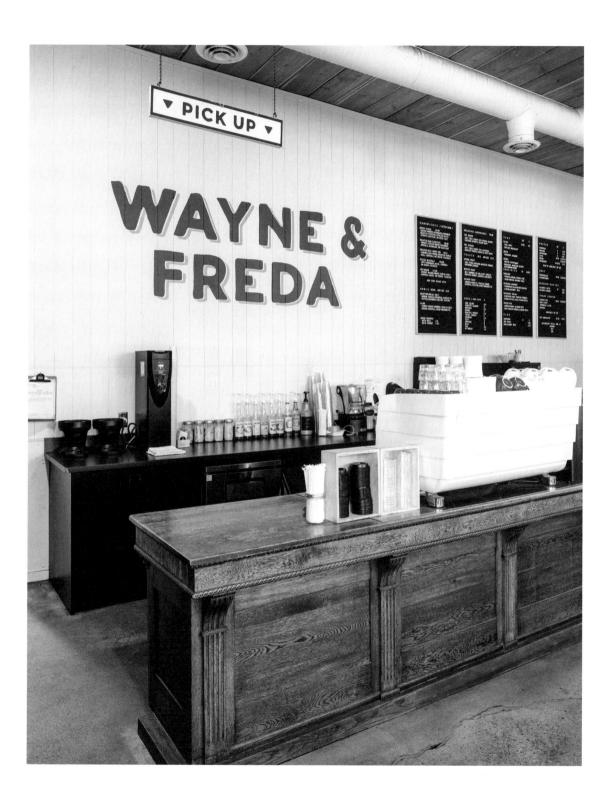

Braised Beef Sandwich with Roasted Garlic and Dijon Aioli

Time Family of Wines
McWatters Collection
Red Meritage

Wayne & Freda is more than just coffee and breakfast pastries; they also do a busy lunch business with salads, bowls and sandwiches like this hearty braised beef on tender focaccia. SERVES 4

BRAISED BEEF

3 Tbsp grainy Dijon mustard
3 Tbsp vegetable oil (divided)
2 Tbsp dried thyme
1 Tbsp salt, plus extra to taste
1 Tbsp black pepper
2 lbs boneless beef short ribs, room temperature
2 large white onions, roughly chopped
2 carrots, roughly chopped
4 stalks celery, roughly chopped
1 cup red wine
10 cloves garlic
5 bay leaves
2 sprigs rosemary
1 pint grape tomatoes
Bunch of parsley stems
Small handful of thyme sprigs
8 to 12 cups well-seasoned beef stock

DIJON AIOLI

1 egg yolk
1 tsp white wine vinegar
Reserved braised garlic (see here)
1 Tbsp grainy Dijon mustard
½ tsp salt
½ tsp black pepper
¼ cup canola oil
¼ cup olive oil

ASSEMBLY

Focaccia, cut into sandwich-size pieces
Salt
Arugula

BRAISED BEEF In a small bowl, combine mustard, 2 tablespoons oil, dried thyme, salt and pepper and mix well. Rub beef with the mixture. Set aside for at least 1 hour.

Heat the remaining tablespoon of oil in a heavy-bottomed frying pan over medium-high heat. Carefully place marinated beef into the pan and brown for 3 to 4 minutes on each side, until golden brown. Transfer to a plate.

Add onions, carrots and celery to the pan and sauté over medium heat for 10 minutes, or until caramelized. (Increase heat if needed.) Transfer vegetables to a plate.

Pour wine into the same pan and deglaze, then reduce heat to low and simmer for 10 to 15 minutes, until reduced by half. Remove from heat.

Preheat oven to 350°F.

Place garlic in a coffee filter or spice bag and tie up with twine to make a bundle.

Transfer beef to a roasting pan or Dutch oven, then add sautéed vegetables, the garlic bundle and wine. Add remaining ingredients and pour in enough stock until the ribs are completely submerged. Cover and braise in the oven for 2 to 4 hours, until beef is fork tender. Season with salt to taste. Remove garlic from bundle and reserve for aioli.

DIJON AIOLI Meanwhile, combine egg yolk, vinegar, braised garlic, mustard, salt and pepper in a bowl and whisk until semi-smooth. (Alternatively, use a food processor.) While constantly whisking, gradually add both oils and blend until emulsified. Chill until ready to serve.

ASSEMBLY Preheat grill over high heat. Toast focaccia lightly on each side. Spread aioli on each slice.

Place a few chunks of short ribs on each sandwich. Sprinkle with a little salt, then top with arugula and close up sandwich.

Double Dark Chocolate Mint Cookies

These cookies remind Jen Hawk of the York Peppermint Patties her grandpa (the Wayne of the café's name) would leave on her pillow at night when she was a little kid. Now a new generation gets to enjoy their darkly comforting chocolatey-mint flavour. MAKES 12 COOKIES

 Dark-Roast Coffee

½ cup (1 stick) butter, room temperature

¾ cup packed demerara-style brown sugar

¼ cup raw sugar

1 egg

1 tsp vanilla extract

1 tsp peppermint extract

1 cup flour

⅓ cup unsweetened cocoa powder

1 tsp dried mint

½ tsp baking soda

¼ tsp salt

8 oz dark chocolate (70% cocoa), chopped

Preheat oven to 350°F. Line 2 baking sheets with parchment paper.

Combine butter and sugars in the bowl of a stand mixer fitted with a paddle attachment. (Or use a hand mixer and bowl.) Cream together for 1 minute, until light and fluffy. Add egg, vanilla and peppermint extract, then mix on medium until fully combined.

In a separate bowl, sift together flour, cocoa powder, mint, baking soda and salt.

With the motor of the mixer running on low speed, add the flour mixture in two additions, scraping down the sides of the bowl after each addition. Mix just until combined. (Do not overmix.) Fold in chocolate.

Scoop a heaping tablespoon of dough onto a prepared baking sheet. Repeat with remaining cookie dough, evenly spacing them 2 inches apart. (Cookies will spread to double their width.) Bake for 12 to 15 minutes, until light and glossy on top and no longer raw. Remove baking sheets from the oven, tap on counter to remove air bubbles and ensure an even spread, and allow to cool.

METRIC CONVERSION CHART

VOLUME

Imperial or U.S.	Metric
⅛ tsp	0.5 mL
¼ tsp	1 mL
½ tsp	2.5 mL
¾ tsp	4 mL
1 tsp	5 mL
½ Tbsp	8 mL
1 Tbsp	15 mL
1½ Tbsp	23 mL
2 Tbsp	30 mL
¼ cup	60 mL
⅓ cup	80 mL
½ cup	125 mL
⅔ cup	165 mL
¾ cup	185 mL
1 cup	250 mL
1¼ cups	310 mL
1⅓ cups	330 mL
1½ cups	375 mL
1⅔ cups	415 mL
1¾ cups	435 mL
2 cups	500 mL
2¼ cups	560 mL
2⅓ cups	580 mL
2½ cups	625 mL
2¾ cups	690 mL
3 cups	750 mL
4 cups / 1 quart	1 L
5 cups	1.25 L
6 cups	1.5 L
7 cups	1.75 L
8 cups	2 L
12 cups	3 L

WEIGHT

Imperial or U.S.	Metric
½ oz	15 g
1 oz	30 g
2 oz	60 g
3 oz	85 g
4 oz (¼ lb)	115 g
5 oz	140 g
6 oz	170 g
7 oz	200 g
8 oz (½ lb)	225 g
9 oz	255 g
10 oz	285 g
11 oz	310 g
12 oz (¾ lb)	340 g
13 oz	370 g
14 oz	400 g
15 oz	425 g
16 oz (1 lb)	450 g
1¼ lbs	570 g
1½ lbs	670 g
2 lbs	900 g
3 lbs	1.4 kg
4 lbs	1.8 kg
5 lbs	2.3 kg
6 lbs	2.7 kg

LIQUID MEASURES

(for alcohol)

Imperial or U.S.	Metric
½ fl oz	15 mL
1 fl oz	30 mL
2 fl oz	60 mL
3 fl oz	90 mL
4 fl oz	120 mL

CANS AND JARS

Imperial or U.S.	Metric
6 oz	170 g
14 oz	398 mL
19 oz	540 mL
28 oz	796 mL

LINEAR

Imperial or U.S.	Metric
⅛ inch	3 mm
¼ inch	6 mm
½ inch	12 mm
¾ inch	2 cm
1 inch	2.5 cm
1¼ inches	3 cm
1½ inches	3.5 cm
1¾ inches	4.5 cm
2 inches	5 cm
2½ inches	6.5 cm
3 inches	7.5 cm
4 inches	10 cm
5 inches	12.5 cm
6 inches	15 cm
7 inches	18 cm
10 inches	25 cm
12 inches (1 foot)	30 cm
13 inches	33 cm
16 inches	41 cm
18 inches	46 cm
24 inches (2 feet)	60 cm
28 inches	70 cm
30 inches	75 cm
6 feet	1.8 m

TEMPERATURE

(for oven temperatures, see chart in next column)

Imperial or U.S.	Metric
90°F	32°C
120°F	49°C
125°F	52°C
130°F	54°C
140°F	60°C
150°F	66°C
155°F	68°C
160°F	71°C
165°F	74°C
170°F	77°C
175°F	80°C
180°F	82°C
190°F	88°C
200°F	93°C
240°F	116°C
250°F	121°C
300°F	149°C
325°F	163°C
350°F	177°C
360°F	182°C
375°F	191°C

OVEN TEMPERATURE

Imperial or U.S.	Metric
200°F	95°C
250°F	120°C
275°F	135°C
300°F	150°C
325°F	160°C
350°F	180°C
375°F	190°C
400°F	200°C
425°F	220°C
450°F	230°C
500°F	260°C
550°F	290°C

BAKING PANS

Imperial or U.S.	Metric
5- × 9-inch loaf pan	2 L loaf pan
9- × 13-inch cake pan	4 L cake pan
11- × 17-inch baking sheet	30- × 45-cm baking sheet

ACKNOWLEDGEMENTS

They say it takes a village, but in this case, it took a whole valley of people to bring this book together. More than that, it was a valley of people juggling the staffing shortages, skyrocketing prices and supply-chain issues that followed the pandemic, not to mention a heat dome, wildfires and untimely cold snaps. We know how challenging these last couple of years have been for B.C.'s wine valleys, and we cannot be more grateful to everyone who, despite all that, made the time to share their stories and their recipes. Thank you.

We especially want to thank the chefs, producers, growers and winemakers who are making the Okanagan, Similkameen and Thompson Valleys such dynamic places to eat, drink and visit.

We also want to thank the team at Figure 1, every one of whom makes it a pleasure to work on an ambitious project like this.

That starts with publisher and president Chris Labonté, managing editor Lara Smith, creative director Naomi MacDougall and designer Teresa Bubela. Special thanks go to the people who made our words sing even when we were feeling a little off-key: editor Michelle Meade, copy editor Pam Robertson and proofreader Breanne MacDonald.

Figure 1 is famous for their beautiful books, and it's impossible to create something as pretty as *Okanagan Eats* without great images. Thank you to photographer Jon Adrian for his stunning portraits, landscapes and food shots. Thank you, too, to food and prop stylist Jenny Adrian, prop stylist Tara Reavie and assistant Candice Wahler.

Special thanks to those who donated props and materials for the photoshoot: Fawdry Homes, Minim Designs Pottery, Arcadia Modern Home, Lexi & Lake, Global Surfaces, Luxury Lime Plaster, John Rousseau Design, Vintage Origami, Wall to Wall and RevitaStone.

Finally, big hugs and gratitude to our families, who've had to share us with this project for the last two—two!—years. We hope the delicious food you got to taste makes up for it. We also feel incredibly lucky to have been able to work together again after all the fun we had on *Island Eats*. We'll celebrate over a bottle of B.C. bubbly later.

JOANNE SASVARI AND DAWN POSTNIKOFF

INDEX

G

ganache topping, for Okanagan delight, 187

GARLIC
confit, easy, 156
mayonnaise, spicy, 121
roasted, and Dijon aioli, braised beef sandwich with, 190, *191*

GASTRIQUE
apricot, 69
thyme-scented, 104

gazpacho, heirloom tomato, *19*, 20–21

gluten-free brownie trifle, 107

GNOCCHI
potato, with venison ragù, *145*, 147
rosemary lamb chops with, 179

GOAT CHEESE
in autumn bruschetta, 163
feta, whipped, 105
in Moroccan dip, 174
and wild mushroom quiche with spring salad, 22–23

Grana Padano, in potato gnocchi with venison ragù, 147

granola, house, 85

grapefruit cordial, 137

green apple and Riesling BBQ sauce, 59

green bell pepper, in gazpacho, 20

grilled Okanagan apples, smoked cheddar and pork burger with, *164*, 165

grilled summer peach and burrata salad, *125*, 126

H

Hakurei turnips and apple jam, arctic char with, 112–13

halibut, roasted B.C., with dill, new potatoes and corn-glazed cauliflower, 168, *169*

ham, in grilled summer peach and burrata salad, 126

HASKAP
-jalapeño jam, baked brie with, 25
sour, Okanagan, 77, *77*

HAZELNUT(S)
crumb, for grilled summer peach and burrata salad, 126
in house granola, 85
in things on toast, 104–5
toasted, French beans, heirloom tomatoes and fresh herbs, steak with, 181

heirloom tomatoes. *See under* tomato(es)

HERB(S). *See also specific herbs*
fresh, French beans, heirloom tomatoes and toasted hazelnuts, steak with, 181
oil and burrata, braised lamb with, 160, *161*
salt, 32
in wild mushroom and goat cheese quiche with spring salad, 22–23

HONEY
-caramelized carrots, poached pears and endive, orchard salad with, *110*, 111
hot, 121
truffle, 33

hot honey, 121

house granola, 85

hummus, preserved lemon, *53*, 55

I

ICE CREAM
Chardonnay, sundae and popcorn, with sablé Breton, sesame miso caramel, caramel popcorn and vegan meringue shards, *37*, 40–41
marmalade, salted caramel and Marcona almonds, Basque-style cheesecake with, 83
red wine, Okanagan fruit clafoutis with, 148

J

JALAPEÑO(S)
candied, 122
-haskap jam, baked brie with, 25
in pepita sauce, 175
in salsa fresca, 21

JAM
apple, and Hakurei turnips, arctic char with, 112–13
haskap-jalapeño, baked brie with, 25

jelly, Porto, chicken liver mousse with, 49

jicama, in aguachile, 72

jus, miso–red wine, red cabbage purée, seared red cabbage and pickled cherries, duck breast with, *135*, 138–39

K

kabocha squash, sweet and spicy, 94

kale, in Okanagan ribollita, 155

L

LAMB
braised, with burrata and herb oil, 160, *161*
chops, rosemary, with gnocchi, 179
merguez, Manila clams and rapini, orecchiette with, 79, 81

lavender lemonade cocktail, *99*, 100

LEEK
in classic bouillabaisse, 51
in Okanagan ribollita, 155
in Okanagan spring asparagus, morel and sunchoke soup, 167
in things on toast, 104–5

LEMON
-ade lavender cocktail, *99*, 100
preserved, hummus, *53*, 55

LEMONGRASS
in beef rendang, 46
in coconut curry broth, 45
cream sauce, 27

LETTUCE
in berry pecan salad with Neverland Apple Crumble tea–infused raspberry vinaigrette, 115
in ponzu steak salad, 122–23
romaine, in charred greens, 39
in spring salad, 23

lime-sesame dressing, 123

liver mousse, chicken, with Porto jelly, 49

M

Manila clams, merguez and rapini, orecchiette with, 79, 81

Marcona almonds, marmalade ice cream and salted caramel, Basque-style cheesecake with, 83

marmalade ice cream, salted caramel and Marcona almonds, Basque-style cheesecake with, 83

mayonnaise, spicy garlic, 121

merguez, Manila clams and rapini, orecchiette with, 79, 81

MERINGUE
shards, vegan, 40
shells, for cherry pavlova Bure, 34

milk chocolate. *See under* chocolate

MINT
cookies, double dark chocolate, 193
in grilled summer peach and burrata salad, 126
in smashed peas, 141
in snap pea bruschetta, 64

MISO
in green apple and Riesling BBQ sauce, 59
-red wine jus, red cabbage purée, seared red cabbage and pickled cherries, duck breast with, *135*, 138–39
-sesame caramel, 41
in steak with French beans, heirloom tomatoes, toasted hazelnuts and fresh herbs, 181

MOREL(S)
mushroom soy, soft farm egg, crispy bits and chives, 182, *183*
Okanagan spring asparagus and sunchoke soup, 167
peas and garden sorrel sauce, spring salmon with pommes Anna and, 127
in wild mushroom and goat cheese quiche with spring salad, 22–23

Moroccan dip, *173*, 174

MOUSSE
chicken liver, with Porto jelly, 49
milk chocolate, with salted caramel, 90, *91*

mozzarella, braised lamb with, 160

MUSHROOMS. *See also* morel(s)
cremini, in Cabernet Franc–braised short ribs, 60
stock, quick, 156

ABOUT THE AUTHORS

DAWN POSTNIKOFF

As co-founder of *Edible Vancouver Island*, Dawn Postnikoff now shares her passion for local food with *Edible* communities across Canada. She is a writer, business owner and restaurateur and co-author of the cookbook *Island Eats*. Dawn loves to play outdoors, travel, sip wine and cook with her family and friends in whatever kitchen she happens to find herself in.

JOANNE SASVARI

Joanne Sasvari is the editor of the magazines *YAM*, *Vitis* and *The Alchemist* and writes about food, drink and travel for *Edible Vancouver*, Destination B.C., *Food & Wine* magazine and various other publications. She is also the author of the IACP-shortlisted book *The Wickaninnish Cookbook*, as well as *Vancouver Eats*, *Island Eats* and *Paprika*. In addition, she is a Canadian Wine Scholar, Level II B.C. Wine Ambassador and certified to Level III by the Wine and Spirits Education Trust.